SCIENCE FOR EXCELLENCE

chemical

LEVEL 4

science

Scottish Schools Science Group

Series Editors:
Nicky Souter, Paul Chambers and Stephen Jeffrey

Authors:
Stephen Jeffrey, John Anderson, Fran Macdonald,
Barry McBride and Paul McCranor

DYNAMIC LEARNING

HODDER GIBSON
AN HACHETTE UK COMPANY

The Publishers would like to thank the following for permission to reproduce copyright material:

Photo credits
Page 7 © The Print Collector/Alamy; Page 25 © Neil McAllister/Alamy; Page 27 top right © SCIENCE PHOTO LIBRARY, top left © DAVID HALPERN/SCIENCE PHOTO LIBRARY, middle © Squareplum/Fotolia.com, bottom © MARTIN BOND/SCIENCE PHOTO LIBRARY; Page 29 © Martyn Chillmaid; Page 32 top left © imagebroker/Alamy, top right © Patrick Koslo/Getty Images, bottom left © Akhilesh Sharma – Fotolia, bottom right © South West Images Scotland/Alamy; Page 33 top right © Dennis "S.K"/ Wikipedia Commons, middle left © Construction Photography/Corbis, middle right © ANDREW LAMBERT PHOTOGRAPHY/ SCIENCE PHOTO LIBRARY, bottom left © John Cooper/Alamy; Page 34 © Pamela McGookin; Page 36 © Pamela McGookin; Page 37 © Pamela McGookin; Page 38 top © Skatebiker/Wikipedia Commons, bottom © Pamela McGookin; Page 39 © GIULIANO BEVILACQUA/Rex Features; Page 40 top left © Evo Mag/Kenny P/Rex Features, top right © Photodisc/Getty Images, bottom left © Walter Bibikow/Getty Images, bottom right © Kevin L Neff/Wikipedia Creative Commons; Page 41 top © Mark Evans/iStockphoto. com, bottom © Roman Milert/Fotolia.com; Page 42 left © Tim Harvey/Alamy, right © Imagestate Media; Page 44 top left © COLIN CUTHBERT/SCIENCE PHOTO LIBRARY, bottom left © Kallista Images/Getty Images, bottom right © SCIENCE PHOTO LIBRARY; Page 45 top left © SHEILA TERRY/SCIENCE PHOTO LIBRARY, top right © Pamela McGookin; Page 46 top © Stocksearch/Alamy, middle © Túrelio/Wikipedia Commons, bottom © Don Farrall/Getty Images; Page 47 top © Stockbyte/Getty Images, bottom © Pamela McGookin; Page 50 top and middle (both) © Pamela McGookin; Page 38 top and middle/Skatebiker © Pamela McGookin, bottom © Roger Bamber/Alamy; Page 51 top © Sinopix/Rex Features, bottom © i love images/Alamy; Page 52 © fine art/Alamy; Page 54 © Pamela McGookin; Page 55 © Hans Kwaspen – Fotolia. com; Page 56 © Pamela McGookin; Page 57 (both) © Pamela McGookin; Page 58 © MARTYN F. CHILLMAID/SCIENCE PHOTO LIBRARY; Page 59 top left © Deglr6328/Wikipedia Commons, top right © Caroline Schiff/Fotolia.com, bottom left © Mikael Karlsson/ Alamy, bottom right © David Shale/Nature Picture Library; Page 64 left © Hodder Gibson, right © Pamela McGookin; Page 65 (both) © Pamela McGookin; Page 69 (both) © Pamela McGookin; Page 78 top and middle right © Pamela McGookin, middle left © Kevin Wheal/Alamy; Page 79 left and middle © NI Syndication, right © Morey Milbradt/Getty Images; Page 81 © 3D Clinic/Getty Images; Page 84 © Pete Oxford/Minden Pictures/FLPA; Page 85 left © ESA – European Space Agency, right © John Stillwell/PA Wire/Press Association Images; Page 86 © Science Museum/ SSPL; Page 89 © Samiylenko/Fotolia.com; Page 90 © slaven gabric/Alamy; Page 95 left © Stockbyte/ Photolibrary Group Ltd, right © Mark Boulton/Alamy; Page 96 © BAKO GABOR/AP/Press Association Images; Page 97 © Andrew Milligan/PA Archive/Press Association Images; Page 98 © Argent Energy (UK) Ltd; Page 99 © Spencer Grant/Alamy; Page 103 top left © ZEPHYR/SCIENCE PHOTO LIBRARY, top right © Enigma/Alamy, bottom (three images) © CHARLES D. WINTERS/SCIENCE PHOTO LIBRARY; Page 104 © NSG Group; Page 105 © Sipa Press/Rex Features; Page 106 © PASIEKA/ SCIENCE PHOTO LIBRARY; Page 107 © LAWRENCE BERKELEY NATIONAL LABORATORY/ SCIENCE PHOTO LIBRARY; Pages 6, 21, 31, 53, 61 and 101 © Photodisc/Getty Images; Page 43 MEDICAL RF.COM/SCIENCE PHOTO LIBRARY; Pages 76 and 88 © Digital Stock.

Acknowledgements
'Oxygen' by Roger McGough from *Defying Gravity* (Copyright © Roger McGough 1992) is reproduced by permission of PFD on behalf of Roger McGough; 'Carbon' by Roger McGough from *Defying Gravity* (Copyright © Roger McGough 1992) is reproduced by permission of PFD on behalf of Roger McGough.

Every effort has been made to trace all copyright holders, but if any have been inadvertently overlooked the Publishers will be pleased to make the necessary arrangements at the first opportunity.

Although every effort has been made to ensure that website addresses are correct at time of going to press, Hodder Gibson cannot be held responsible for the content of any website mentioned in this book. It is sometimes possible to find a relocated web page by typing in the address of the home page for a website in the URL window of your browser.

Hachette UK's policy is to use papers that are natural, renewable and recyclable products and made from wood grown in sustainable forests. The logging and manufacturing processes are expected to conform to the environmental regulations of the country of origin.

Whilst every effort has been made to check the instructions of practical work in this book, it is still the duty and legal obligation of schools to carry out their own risk assessments.

Orders: please contact Bookpoint Ltd, 130 Milton Park, Abingdon, Oxon OX14 4SB. Telephone: (44) 01235 827720. Fax: (44) 01235 400454. Lines are open 9.00–5.00, Monday to Saturday, with a 24-hour message answering service. Visit our website at www. hoddereducation.co.uk. Hodder Gibson can be contacted direct on: Tel: 0141 848 1609; Fax: 0141 889 6315; email: hoddergibson@ hodder.co.uk.

© Scottish Schools Science Group 2011
First published in 2011 by
Hodder Gibson, an imprint of Hodder Education,
An Hachette UK Company
2a Christie Street
Paisley PA1 1NB

Impression number   5 4 3 2
Year   2014 2013

Cover photo © Photodisc/Getty Images
Illustrations by Emma Golley at Redmoor Design, Tony Wilkins and DC Graphic Design Limited
Typeset in Minion 12/15pt by DC Graphic Design Limited, Swanley, Kent
Printed in Dubai

A catalogue record for this title is available from the British Library

ISBN: 978 1444 145 229

Contents

Introduction

Science for Excellence Level 4: Chemical Science is directed towards the Level Four Science experiences and outcomes of Curriculum for Excellence in Scotland. Its main focus is on those relating to Planet Earth and Materials. It makes frequent reference to key concepts identified in Curriculum for Excellence and the topics chosen in the text can be linked with content across the other organisers.

Although the chapters are designed to meet Curriculum for Excellence Level Four outcomes, their approach and content have also been influenced by the need to articulate with National Four and National Five developments which were underway at the time of writing. An enquiry-based approach suggests activities which are designed to encourage pupils to plan and design experiments which present opportunities for individual investigation or practical challenges but also others which are more designed to provide progression onto the next stage. This is reflected in the inclusion of content covering, for example, novel materials and nanotechnology.

In an attempt to allow our pupils to make more informed decisions on scientific issues relating to their own experiences, the chapters have a strong Scottish viewpoint, but this is balanced by reference to global issues. It is hoped that the chemical science content, presented alongside examples of historical ideas will develop pupils' awareness of science as a continuing process involving tentative ideas, and that what is considered correct at one time may be refined in light of new discoveries.

Some of the activities in the book involve experiments. These should only be attempted under the instruction of the Science Teacher and in accordance with the appropriate safety guidelines. Problems and activities are designed to examine and extend the content of the chapters. Skills in literacy and numeracy as well as an awareness of the importance of health and wellbeing will be developed through these exercises – look out for the icons shown at the end of this Introduction. Some chapters allow for numerical and graphical activities where others seek to reinforce the scientific principles contained in the main text. It was also felt that in an attempt to make the learners more active participants, open ended and pupil investigation activities should feature. These activities encourage individual project work, research and group work, with learners being asked to make informed decisions on scientific advances which may have ethical or societal implications. The tasks are designed around the "broad features of assessment in science".

The principles and practices outlined in Curriculum for Excellence have been adopted throughout the *Science for Excellence* series. The series is designed to be used in conjunction with schemes of work which reflect learning and teaching approaches which are most applicable to the sciences.

The series provides opportunities for scientific enquiry and examples of scientific scenarios where pupils can, for example, link variables to determine relationships or improve their scientific thinking or make informed judgements on the basis of scientific principles.

Scientifically Literate Citizens

The series' use of real data and experimental type situations are designed to support the development of pupils' scientific attitudes. They will be able to look at data critically, make informed judgements on the basis of these and be critical and analytical of the science as well as the implications of broad or bold claims. Our scientific and technological development in various areas and at various times is recorded, and the impact of those developments is seen in context and as an indication of how our society has used and managed science for our benefit.

A significant challenge for Curriculum for Excellence and the *Science for Excellence* series is to change our pupils' attitudes to science and to help them become more able to engage positively in issues that will affect them. It is intended that the series' approach and content will help them to appreciate the scientific challenges and issues facing mankind and to respond in critical and informed ways.

Science for Excellence strives to act as a sound preparatory text for all pupils, including those progressing to the next stage, providing a secure understanding of the key issues in science.

 Literacy

 Numeracy

 Health and wellbeing

MATERIALS
Properties and uses of substances

1

Bonding, structure and properties

Level 3 — What came before?

SCN 3-15a

I have developed my knowledge of the Periodic Table by considering the properties and uses of a variety of elements relative to their positions.

Level 4 — What is this chapter about?

SCN 4-15a

Through gaining an understanding of the structure of atoms and how they join, I can begin to connect the properties of substances with their possible structures.

Bonding, structure and properties

The atom

In Level 3 we looked at the **atom** and the suggestions made about the atom by John Dalton, the English chemist who is famous for his work in the development of understanding of the nature of the atom.

Dalton suggested that:

1 **Elements** are made from tiny particles called atoms.

2 All the atoms of an element are identical.

3 The atoms of one element are different from the atoms of any other element.

4 Atoms of one element can join with atoms of another element to form **compounds**.

In this chapter we are going to concentrate on the fourth point made by Dalton: the fact that atoms can join together to make millions of different compounds, all of which have different chemical and physical properties. The properties that compounds have are determined by the type of **bonds** that hold the atoms together.

To understand fully the bonds that hold atoms together we must look again at the structure of the atom.

Atoms are made up of three small particles called electrons, protons and neutrons.

Electrons are negatively charged particles that orbit around the positive centre of the atom in energy levels. Their mass is so small it is nearly zero.

Protons are positively charged particles that are contained in the nucleus of the atom. They have a mass of 1 amu (atomic mass unit).

Neutrons are also contained in the nucleus of the atom but have no charge. They also have a mass of 1 amu.

Overall, atoms have a neutral charge. This is because they have the same number of positive protons and negative electrons. These opposite charges cancel each other out making the atom neutral overall.

Each element in the **Periodic Table** has its own **atomic number**. The atomic number is equal to the number of protons in the atom. Calcium has the atomic number of 20; this means that calcium atoms contain 20 protons.

John Dalton

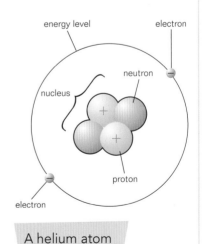

A helium atom

The atom

QUESTIONS

1 An atom contains negatively and positively charged particles.

   a) What are the negative and positive particles called?

   b) What is the overall charge of the nucleus?

   c) Explain your answer to b).

   d) What is the overall charge of an atom?

   e) Explain your answer to d).

   f) Sketch the structure of the atom to show where the negative and positive particles are found.

2 In 1932 a third particle was discovered in the atom.

   a) Name the third particle.

   b) What charge does this particle have?

   c) Do some research to discover the name of the scientist who discovered this particle and explain why it was more difficult to find than electrons and protons.

3 The information in this section can be summarised into a table. Copy and complete the table below.

Particle	Charge	Mass	Location in the atom
	positive		
		0	energy level
		1	nucleus

How atoms combine

Now that we know what an atom is, we have to learn about how these atoms combine and what holds them together when compounds form.

Covalent bonding

The Noble Gases are like the pop stars or sport stars of the Periodic Table. All the other elements in the Periodic Table aspire to be like them. This is why the Noble Gases do not react with other elements – they do not want to be changed in any way. They are perfect just the way they are. In chemistry terms they are said to be stable.

The reason for this is that atoms of the Noble Gases have a stable **electron arrangement**. The electron arrangement of an atom refers to the number of electrons in each energy level; this information can be found in some Periodic Tables or data booklets. If you look them up, you will find that, apart from helium, all Noble Gas electron arrangements end in 8. This tells us that the outer energy level of each Noble Gas is filled with electrons – there is no room for any more to be added. Helium atoms only have two electrons, and these fill the first energy level. As a result, the electron arrangement of helium is 2. For all other elements, however, this is not the case. Carbon atoms, for example,

How atoms combine

have six electrons, giving the electron arrangement 2, 4. This tells us that two electrons are in the first energy level and four are in the second.

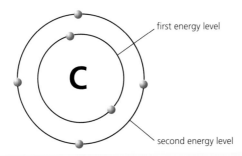

The electron arrangement of a carbon atom

The first energy level can hold a maximum of two electrons and the second and third energy levels can hold a maximum of eight. This can be seen in the Noble Gas argon, which has the electron arrangement 2, 8, 8.

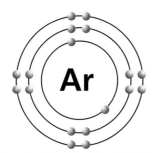

The electron arrangement of an argon atom

If atoms of other elements are to become stable like those of the Noble Gases, they must try to achieve an electron arrangement like a Noble Gas, meaning a full outer energy level. There are two ways in which atoms can do this: by **sharing** electrons with other atoms or by electrons being **transferred** between atoms. These things happen when atoms join up or bond with others. We shall look first at bonds called **covalent bonds**.

A covalent bond is a shared pair of electrons between two non-metal atoms.

Non-metal atoms often bond covalently, forming **molecules**. The atoms within the molecule are held together because of the force of attraction between the positive nucleus of each atom and the negatively charged shared pairs of electrons.

How atoms combine

This is better illustrated as a diagram.

The saying 'opposites attract' can be used to describe how covalent bonding works. The positively charged nucleus of each atom is attracted to the negatively charged shared pair of electrons. This is known as an **electrostatic** force of attraction and is shown by the dashed lines in the diagram. This creates a 'tug-of-war' effect. Both nuclei try to pull the shared electrons towards themselves creating a strong bond that holds the atoms together.

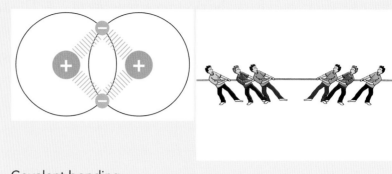
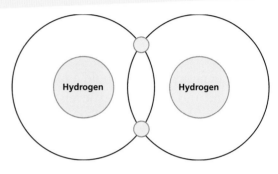

Covalent bonding

Shown here is a molecule of hydrogen. Hydrogen atoms have the electron arrangement of 1; in other words, hydrogen atoms have only one electron. So if one hydrogen atom shares its electron with that of another atom of hydrogen, they now share two outer electrons, which gives them the same stable electron arrangement as the Noble Gas helium.

A hydrogen molecule

QUESTIONS

1 Explain why an atom reacts and forms a covalent bond with another atom and explain how a covalent bond holds these atoms together.

2 In which of the following compounds are the atoms held together by covalent bonds? (Hint: Look at the definition of a covalent bond.)

   sodium chloride, water, carbon dioxide, lithium fluoride, sulphur dioxide, carbon hydride, aluminium oxide, carbon tetrachloride, calcium carbonate

3 Look at the electron arrangements of all the elements in Group 1. What feature of their electron arrangement makes them react in similar ways?

4 Copy and complete the table below and draw diagrams to show how the electrons are arranged in each of the elements.

Element	Number of electrons	Electron arrangement
nitrogen	7	2, 5
magnesium		2, 8, 2
	17	2, 8, 7
neon		
lithium	3	

Diatomic molecules

As previously mentioned, when two or more non-metal atoms join together they form molecules. A **diatomic molecule** is a molecule that contains two atoms. There are several elements that exist as diatomic molecules. All of them are listed below. To make it easy to remember all the diatomic elements, use this little **mnemonic** or make up your own.

Fancy	Fluorine	F_2
Clancy	Chlorine	Cl_2
Owes	Oxygen	O_2
Him	Hydrogen	H_2
Nothing	Nitrogen	N_2
But	Bromine	Br_2
Ice	Iodine	I_2

Oxygen is a diatomic molecule; that is why its formula is O_2.

The diatomic elements exist this way as it allows them to achieve a stable outer energy level like a Noble Gas. A diagram showing how the outer electrons are arranged can be drawn for all the diatomic elements. The example below is fluorine.

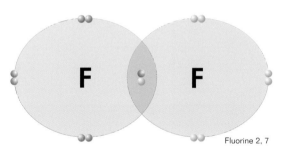

Fluorine 2, 7

The electron arrangement for the diatomic element fluorine

This diagram shows a molecule of fluorine. An atom of fluorine requires one electron to become stable like a Noble Gas and therefore it will share one electron with another atom of fluorine to form two stable atoms.

An oxygen atom has the electron arrangement 2, 6 and requires two electrons to become stable. Because of this it must share two electrons with another oxygen atom. This means that oxygen forms a double covalent bond.

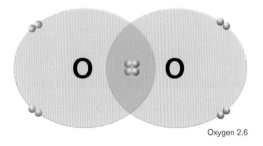

Oxygen 2,6

An oxygen molecule

To make sure you have drawn the diagrams correctly, just count the electrons. With the exception of hydrogen, each atom should have eight electrons. Hydrogen will only have two electrons, as this fills the first energy level.

How atoms combine

QUESTIONS

1 The element iodine exists as a diatomic molecule.

   a) What is meant by the term diatomic?

   b) What is it that holds the iodine molecule together?

   c) Draw a diagram to show how the outer electrons in iodine atoms combine to form an iodine molecule.

2 The grid below shows six molecules.

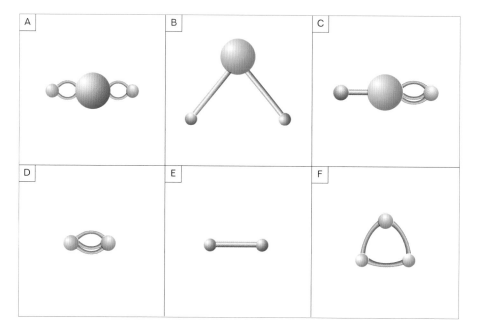

   a) Which boxes show diatomic elements?

   b) Which box could represent hydrogen?

   c) Which box could represent nitrogen?

Chemical formulae

H_2O, CO_2, MgO, Al_2O_3 – where do chemists get these formulae from? The formulae for compounds have actually been worked out from the results of experiments. However, there is a short cut and it is quite easy if you can understand the idea of **valency**.

Chemical formulae

Every element has a valency, although many elements have more than one! Valency is the number of bonds that an atom of an element can form with other atoms. Imagine that valency is like an arm; if an element has a valency of 1 then it has one arm. For example:

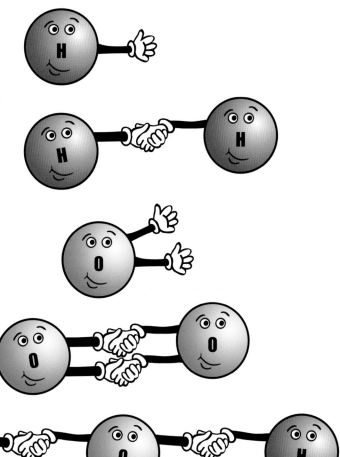

Hydrogen has a valency of 1 and can therefore make one bond.

Oxygen has a valency of 2 and can make two bonds.

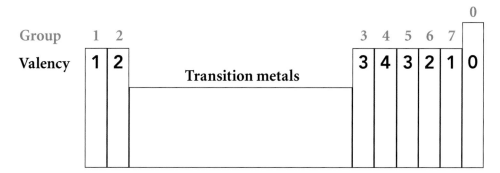

The valency of an element can be established using the Periodic Table as shown below. This means, for example, that all the Alkali Metals in Group 1 of the Table have a valency of 1.

Group	1	2			3	4	5	6	7	0
Valency	1	2	**Transition metals**		3	4	3	2	1	0

The valency of a transition metal in a compound is shown using the Roman Numerals I, II, III and IV for 1, 2, 3 and 4 in brackets after the name of the metal; for example silver (I) oxide, copper (II) chloride, iron (III) sulphate, etc. The valency for 'sulphate' in the last example will be covered later (see 'Working out formulae containing chemical groups' on this page).

To write a chemical formula it is best to use the **SVSDF** system. This is how to use it to work out the formula of carbon dioxide:

Symbols	C	O	
Valencies	4	2	(from the Periodic Table)
Swap	2	4	
Divide	1	2	(divide by the smaller number)
Formula	CO_2		(the '1' is not included in the formula)

When dividing, always use the smaller number. If the numbers do not divide into each other then miss this stage out. Here is another example, which shows how to work out the formula for nitrogen hydride (ammonia):

Symbols	N	H
Valency	3	1
Swap	1	3
Formula	NH_3	

The above two compounds are covalent – they contain atoms of non-metal elements only. However, the SVSDF method can also be used to work out formulae for compounds containing metals. Here are two examples – potassium oxide and magnesium oxide:

Symbols	K	O
Valencies	1	2
Swap	2	1
Formula	K_2O	

Symbols	Mg	O
Valencies	2	2
Swap	2	2
Divide	1	1
Formula	MgO	

Working out formulae containing chemical groups

How do you write formulae for compounds which contain more than two elements, such as sodium hydroxide, calcium carbonate, copper (II) sulphate, etc? Hydroxide, carbonate and sulphate are examples of **groups** which have formulae and valencies all of their own! Hydroxide has the formula OH and a valency of 1, carbonate has the formula CO_3 and a valency of 2 and sulphate has the formula SO_4 and also has a valency of 2. You do not need to memorise these – formulae and valencies for groups can be found in chemistry data booklets. Once you know that, it is as easy as SVSDF!

First, sodium hydroxide:

Symbols	Na	OH
Valencies	1	1
Swap	1	1
Formula	NaOH	

Now calcium carbonate:

Symbols	Ca	CO_3
Valencies	2	2
Swap	2	2
Divide	1	1
Formula	$CaCO_3$	

And finally copper (II) sulphate:

Symbols	Cu	SO_4
Valencies	2	2
Swap	2	2
Divide	1	1
Formula	$CuSO_4$	

A trickier example

What is the formula for calcium hydroxide?

Symbols   Ca   OH
Valencies   2   1
Swap   1   2

At this stage, we need to write a formula which contains two hydroxide groups. To write $CaOH_2$ would be incorrect because that '2' applies only to the 'H' and not the 'O'. We get around this by using **brackets**.

Formula $Ca(OH)_2$

Remember this when writing formulae for compounds which contain groups.

Another short cut!

Sometimes the name of a compound allows you to write its formula without even using SVSDF! Carbon dioxide has the formula CO_2 – **di**oxide indicates two atoms of oxygen. The table below lists some examples of these types of compounds.

Compound	Formula	Prefix
carbon monoxide	CO	mono = 1
sulphur dioxide	SO_2	di = 2
nitrogen trihydride	NH_3	tri = 3
carbon tetrachloride	CCl_4	tetra = 4
phosphorus pentachloride	PCl_5	penta = 5

QUESTIONS

1   Copy the following table and use the Periodic Table to work out the formula for each compound.

Compound name	Formula
hydrogen chloride	
calcium bromide	
aluminium fluoride	
aluminium sulphide	
sodium chloride	
mercury (II) oxide	
iron (III) chloride	
silicon dioxide	

2   Compound X is known to bond covalently with fluorine to form a compound with the formula XF_2. In this compound both X and fluorine attain Noble Gas electron arrangements by sharing electrons.

a) To which group in the Periodic Table is X likely to belong?

b) Draw a diagram to show how the outer electrons are shared to form the covalent bonds in XF_2.

c) With which Noble Gas does fluorine achieve the same electron arrangement as in the compound XF_2?

Numeracy   + − ÷ ×

Find out which numbers the Roman Numerals C, D, L, M and X represent. Have you ever noticed these letters being used at the end of some television programmes and films? For example, a programme made in 2010 would show MMX, one made in 2009 would show MMIX and one made in 2011 would show MMXI. Can you see why? If so, perhaps you can 'translate' these Roman Numerals into numbers:

MMV   MCM   MCMLXVII   MD   MDCLXVI

Shapes of molecules

Certain molecules have specific shapes due to repulsion between electrons. You already know that particles with the same charge move away from (repel) each other. Inside molecules, covalent bonds (shared pairs of electrons) will move as far away from each other as possible. This results in molecules having the shapes shown below. Your teacher may let you use molecular model kits to build these molecules.

Tetrahedral

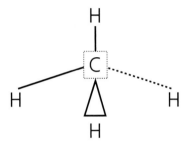

Molecules which have a formula like methane (CH_4), where one atom of one element is joined to four of another, will have this shape. For example, $SiCl_4$ will also be tetrahedral.

Pyramidal

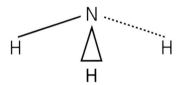

Molecules which have a formula like ammonia (NH_3), where one atom of one element is joined to three of another, will usually have this shape. For example, PH_3 will also be pyramidal.

Bent or V-shaped

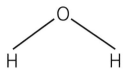

Molecules which have a formula like water (H_2O), where one atom of one element is joined to two of another, will usually have this shape. For example, H_2S will also be V-shaped or bent.

Linear

All diatomic (two atom) molecules, like hydrogen fluoride (HF) shown above, are linear.

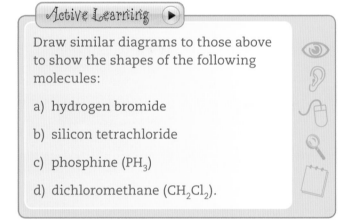

Active Learning

Draw similar diagrams to those above to show the shapes of the following molecules:

a) hydrogen bromide

b) silicon tetrachloride

c) phosphine (PH_3)

d) dichloromethane (CH_2Cl_2).

Ionic bonding

Ionic bonds are the electrostatic forces of attraction between positive ions and negative ions.

An **ion** is a charged particle (in the same way as a proton has a positive charge and an electron has a negative charge).

Forming ions

Atoms become stable by achieving the same electron arrangement as Noble Gases which have full energy levels. We have already seen that non-metal atoms do this by sharing electrons. In contrast, metal atoms do this by **losing** electrons.

Sodium atoms have the electron arrangement 2, 8, 1. A sodium atom will become stable if it loses its outer electron leaving the new outer energy level with eight electrons – like a Noble Gas! However, this creates an imbalance in the atom. Sodium atoms are neutral because they have 11 positive protons and 11 negative electrons. When they lose an electron, they are no longer neutral because they have 11 positive protons but only 10 negative electrons. The atom has become an ion with a single positive charge:

$$\text{Na} \quad \rightarrow \quad \text{Na}^+ \quad + \quad e^-$$

2, 8, 1	2, 8	
sodium atom	sodium ion	lost electron

All Group 1 metal atoms form ions with a single positive charge by losing the one electron which they have in the outer energy level. Atoms of other metals have more than one outer electron. They form ions by losing **all** of their outer electrons and the ions formed can, for example, be double positive (2+) or triple positive (3+). For Group 2 metals like magnesium, this happens:

$$\text{Mg} \quad \rightarrow \quad \text{Mg}^{2+} \quad + \quad 2e^-$$

2, 8, 2	2, 8	
magnesium atom	magnesium ion	two lost electrons

For Group 3:

$$\text{Al} \quad \rightarrow \quad \text{Al}^{3+} \quad + \quad 3e^-$$

2, 8, 3	2, 8	
aluminium atom	aluminium ion	three lost electrons

Non-metal atoms form ions by **gaining** enough electrons to fill their outer energy level. For Group 7 elements, which all have seven outer electrons, this is achieved by gaining one electron. The ion produced

has one more negative electron than positive protons and so has a single negative charge. For example:

$$\text{Cl} \quad + \quad e^- \quad \rightarrow \quad \text{Cl}^-$$

2, 8, 7		2, 8, 8
chlorine atom	gained electron	chlor**ide** ion

Note that the negative ion is named differently from the atom – it has become 'chloride' rather than 'chlorine'. This is always the case when non-metal atoms form ions.

For Group 6 elements, which all have six outer electrons, ions are formed by gaining two electrons. The ion produced has two more negative electrons than positive protons and so has a double negative (2–) charge. For example:

$$\text{O} \quad + \quad 2e^- \quad \rightarrow \quad \text{O}^{2-}$$

2, 6		2, 8
oxygen atom	two gained electrons	ox**ide** ion

For Group 5 elements, which all have five outer electrons, ions are formed by gaining three electrons. The ion produced has three more negative electrons than positive protons and so has a triple negative (3–) charge. For example:

$$\text{P} \quad + \quad 3e^- \quad \rightarrow \quad \text{P}^{3-}$$

2, 8, 5		2, 8, 8
phosphorus atom	three gained electrons	phosph**ide** ion

When metals react with non-metals, electrons lost by the metal atom are picked up by the non-metal atom – this creates both positive and negative ions. These oppositely charged ions are then attracted to each other like the opposite ends of a magnet and ionic bonds are formed between the two sets of ions.

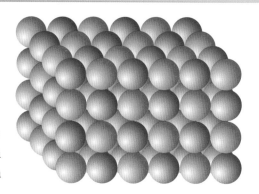

This results in the formation of what is known as an **ionic lattice** structure like the one shown on the right.

If this is a sodium chloride lattice, then each red ball could be a sodium ion and each blue ball a chloride ion. Note that we do not try to count the number of ions in the lattice when we write the formula for sodium chloride. NaCl (or Na^+Cl^-) does not mean **one** sodium ion and **one** chloride ion. It means that the **ratio** of sodium ions to chloride ions in the lattice is 1:1. This is quite different from covalent compounds whose formulae usually show how many atoms are in one molecule of the substance.

QUESTIONS

1 Classify the compounds below as ionic or covalent. Copy and complete the table, entering the name of each compound beneath the correct heading.

sodium chloride, water, potassium bromide, nitrogen iodide, carbon dioxide, lithium fluoride, sulphur dioxide, carbon hydride, aluminium oxide, carbon tetrachloride

Ionic compound	Covalent compound

2 When calcium atoms form ions, two outer electrons are lost producing an ion with a 2+ charge:

$$Ca \rightarrow Ca^{2+} + 2e^-$$
$$2, 8, 8, 2 \qquad 2, 8, 8$$

Write similar equations for the following elements – remember that non-metal atoms gain electrons!

a) potassium

b) sulphur

c) fluorine

d) aluminium

Properties of ionic compounds

As mentioned above, the ions in ionic compounds pack together in what is known as a lattice structure. This is a very stable structure and is the reason why ionic compounds are solid at room temperature and have very high melting points. It takes lots of energy to overcome the strong forces of attraction between the ions in the lattice (the ionic bonds) so that the solid can melt and become a liquid. When ionic compounds have been melted, the ions become free to move and so these compounds can conduct electricity when molten. Many ionic compounds are also soluble in water. Again, this allows the ions to move and so solutions of ionic compounds can also conduct electricity.

$\Rightarrow$

Properties of covalent compounds

Most covalent compounds are made of small molecules which contain the numbers of atoms of each element indicated in the formula. HCl has two atoms, CO_2 has three, CH_4 has five, $C_6H_{12}O_6$ has 24 and so on. Such compounds are said to be **discrete molecular** compounds – each molecule exists somewhat separately and is only loosely attracted to other molecules of the same kind. While the covalent bonds inside these molecules which hold them together are strong, only weak forces of attraction exist between them.

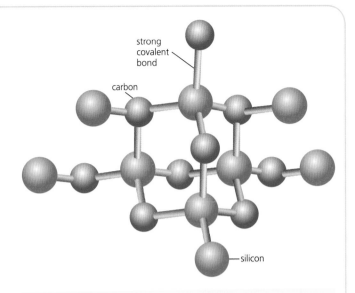

The covalent network structure of silicon carbide

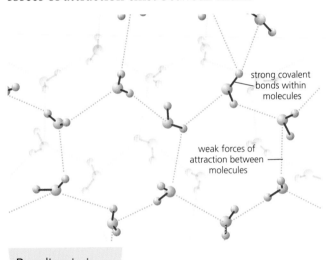

Bonding in ice

As a result, covalent compounds have low melting points. Ice, sugar, fat and wax are easy to melt. This is because it is not the covalent bonds inside their molecules which need to be broken – it is the weak forces of attraction between the molecules. When discrete molecular covalent compounds have been melted, the molecules become free to move. Molten covalent compounds **do not** conduct electricity, however, because molecules are not charged particles – an electric current is a flow of charged particles. Some covalent compounds are soluble in water, but these solutions do not conduct electricity either for the same reason.

A small number of covalent compounds have a quite different structure known as a **covalent network**. These are solids at room temperature and have a structure which looks a bit like an ionic lattice.

Covalent networks are massive molecules with a huge number of atoms. Just as with ionic lattices, their formulae show the ratio of atoms present, not the exact number of each. Silicon carbide has the formula SiC – the ratio of silicon atoms to carbon atoms in the network is 1:1.

Covalent network substances have very high melting points because all of the strong covalent bonds would have to be broken to make the solid become a liquid. They are also very hard. Silicon carbide, for example, is used in tools for cutting through rock.

Bonding, structure and properties

QUESTIONS

Chemical X is being studied to try to establish what type of bonds it contains. The results obtained are recorded below.

Test	Result
solubility in water	very soluble
melting point	high
conduction	only when molten or in solution

Suggest what type of bonding exists in chemical X.

GLOSSARY

Atom a particle made up of protons, neutrons and electrons

Atomic number the number given to each atom in the Periodic Table; it is equal to the number of protons in the atom

Compound two or more elements chemically joined

Covalent bond an electrostatic force of attraction resulting from two atoms sharing a pair of electrons

Covalent network a giant structure containing atoms held together by covalent bonds; they have very high melting points

Diatomic molecules a molecule made up of two atoms such as O_2 or CO

Electron a negatively charged particle with a mass of 0; it is located in the energy levels of an atom

Electrostatic the attractive force between oppositely charged particles

Element contains only one type of atom

Ion a charged particle

Ionic bond an electrostatic force of attraction formed between positive ions and negative ions

Ionic lattice a large arrangement of ions held together by ionic bonds

Molecule two or more atoms held together by covalent bonds

Neutron a neutral particle found in the nucleus of an atom; it has a mass of 1

Proton a positively charged particle found in the nucleus of an atom; it has a mass of 1

Valency the number of bonds that an atom can form with other atoms

MATERIALS
Earth's materials

Carbon – the clever element

Level 3 — What came before?

 SCN 3-17b

I can participate in practical activities to extract useful substances from natural resources.

Level 4 — What is this chapter about?

 SCN 4-17a

I have explored how different materials can be derived from crude oil and their uses. I can explain the importance of carbon compounds in our lives.

 SCN 4-04b

Through investigation, I can explain the formation and use of fossil fuels and contribute to discussions on the responsible use and conservation of finite resources.

Carbon – the clever element

Fossil fuels: the origins

The three main fossil fuels are coal, crude oil and natural gas. The word 'fossil' is used because it takes millions of years for these fuels to form. They are said to be 'finite' resources because they will at some point run out, so we had better not waste them.

Fossil fuels are made from dead **organic** matter that has sunk into the Earth's crust and decayed in the absence of any oxygen (air) under great pressure and at high temperatures for millions of years.

QUESTIONS

1 Find the name of the fourth substance which can be described as a 'fossil' fuel.

2 What is a fuel?

3 What do all fuels combine with when they burn?

Coal

Coal tends to be found in layers, or 'seams', where tree ferns and other plants from huge **prehistoric** forests sank into swamps and were covered by mud and silt.

Uses of coal

All three fossil fuels are burned to produce energy, but they can have much wider uses. If coal is heated to around 2000 °C in the absence of air (so it does not catch fire) all the **volatile** compounds evaporate leaving a smokeless fuel called coke. There are around 200 of these volatile compounds (about 25% of the mass of most types of coal) and they are collected in two main groups: coal tar and coal gas. Coal tar contains some of the chemicals that were used in the nineteenth century to make the first dyes and antiseptics and it still has a variety of medicinal uses. Coke is used widely in the extraction of iron from its ore and in the manufacture of steel.

Active Learning

1 Research the history of coal mining in Scotland.

- How long have we had working mines in Scotland?

- Which were the main coal-producing areas?

- How many working mines were open at the peak of the industry?

- How many are still open?

- Give a reason for the decline in Scottish mining.

2 Find out what 'Perkin's mauve' was and why it was so important in the history of our consumer culture. Write a short newspaper article for *The Scotsman* of 1857 describing the new discovery and the impact it made on society.

Crude oil

Crude oil is by far the most versatile of all the fossil fuels. It is found today under land which was once covered by prehistoric oceans or beneath what is still the sea bed, as is the case in the North Sea off the north coast of Scotland. It formed from sea creatures and plants which died and sank to the bottom of the oceans and were covered by sand and silt.

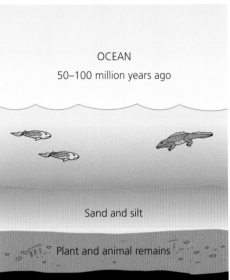
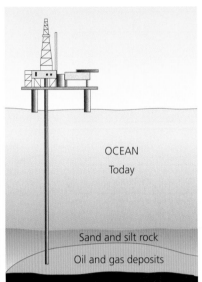

The formation of crude oil and natural gas

Crude oil is a liquid so it gradually collected in soft, **porous**, **sedimentary** rocks formed from the original sand and silt. Often harder, non-porous rock covered the soft rock and, over a very long period of time, the pressure of liquid oil, under its 'cap' of hard rock, built up. When a new oil field is found, drilling through the cap rock releases the pressure and, if great care is not taken, oil can gush uncontrollably out of the new well. In some parts of the world, oil deposits were not covered by hard rock and oil used to seep naturally out of the ground. The surface oil which was found in Pennsylvania, USA, in the nineteenth century started the American oil industry. In its natural state, crude oil is a thick, sticky mixture of solids, liquids and a few gases. Most of the compounds in crude oil are **hydrocarbons** and in the past 100 years, scientists have found an amazing number of uses for this raw material. In its natural state, crude oil is pretty useless, but because all the compounds in crude oil have different boiling points, they can be separated into groups of compounds called **fractions** by a process called **fractional distillation**. The details of this process were covered in Level 3, so you know that these fractions have very familiar names like petrol, diesel and kerosene.

Carbon – the clever element

Carbon compounds derived from crude oil

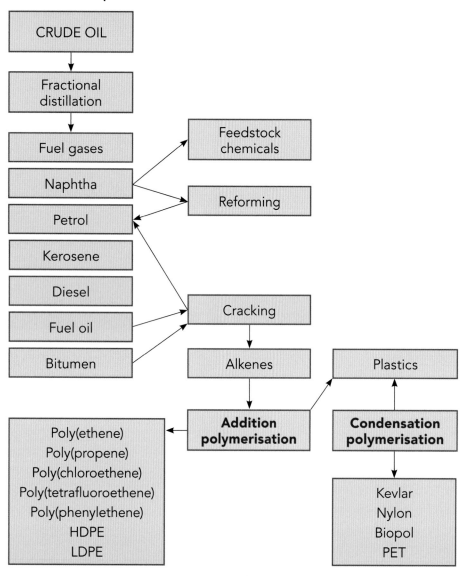

Carbon – the unique element

Carbon has one amazing property; a property that all life depends on – **catenation**! This word means that carbon atoms can combine together to form long chains or rings. No other element on this Earth can undergo catenation to the same extent as carbon. If carbon did not have this property, we would not have sugar, petrol, bread or plastic bags. Perhaps we do not need any of these things, but without catenation, we would not have muscles or DNA either. We are carbon-based life-forms and carbon is the chosen element because it has the property of catenation.

The ability to form rings and very long chains means that there are thousands of carbon compounds and it means that carbon can form some very complicated molecules, from deoxyribonucleic acid (DNA) to polyethylene terephthalate (PET). DNA occurs naturally whereas PET is a synthetic (made in a lab) chemical. Next time you pick up a bottle of water or fizzy juice, you will probably be holding a PET container in your hand. Change the 'ethylene' to 'butylene' and you have PBT. Blend PBT with the stuff DVDs and CDs are made from (polycarbonate, PC) and you have a material which, until recently, was used to make car bumpers.

All the synthetic compounds mentioned so far (PET, PBT and PC) are what the newspapers call 'plastics' and what chemists call **polymers**. The development and manufacture of polymers is a massive growth industry. One polymer can have many very different uses: almost all soft drinks bottles are made from PET, and so are carpets, sails for yachts and thermal fleeces. Most plastics we use every day are blends of two or more polymers that have been 'customised' for specific tasks.

All this sounds complicated, but the creation of these compounds is based on a set of fairly straightforward rules. Developments in chemistry are moving very fast indeed, but the basics stay the same. Anyone who gets a grip on the basics can understand the developments and understand a lot about the world around them.

Active Learning

1 What is the recycling code for PET?

2 Design a poster giving as much information as you can about the meaning of recycling codes: try to find out about the codes for the polymers (or blends of polymers) you can see in the room around you.

3 Which polymer is used to make car tyres and can it be recycled?

Carbon compounds found in crude oil

Most of the compounds found in crude oil are hydrocarbons – compounds that contain the elements carbon and hydrogen only. In Chapter 1 of this book you learned about valency. Carbon has a valency of 4 and hydrogen has a valency of 1, so it would be reasonable to assume that there is only one hydrocarbon compound, CH_4, methane. In fact, because carbon can form long chains and rings of atoms (and because two carbon atoms can be joined by one, two or even three covalent bonds) there are thousands of different hydrocarbon compounds. To make life easier, scientists group these compounds into 'families', usually called **homologous series**. All members of the same series have similar chemical properties, so we can study the properties of a series by experimenting on one member rather than having to study each separate compound.

Carbon – the clever element

Carbon compounds found in crude oil

Most of the hydrocarbons found in crude oil are members of the **alkane** series. Each compound is named according to the number of carbon atoms in one of its molecules, followed by the letters –ane, to show the compound is an alkane. The prefixes used to show the number of carbon atoms are based on Greek words, so they are a bit unusual.

Number of carbon atoms in each molecule	Prefix	Name of alkane	What the molecule looks like (called the structure of the molecule)	Formula
one C atom	meth	methane	H–C–H (with H above and below)	CH_4
two C atoms	eth	ethane		C_2H_6
three C atoms	prop	propane	H–C–C–C–H (with H above and below each C)	
four C atoms	but	butane		C_4H_{10}
five C atoms	pent	pentane	H–C–C–C–C–C–H (with H above and below each C)	
six C atoms	hex	hexane		C_6H_{14}
seven C atoms	hept	heptane	H–C–C–C–C–C–C–C–H (with H above and below each C)	
eight C atoms	oct	octane		C_8H_{18}

The alkane series

Active Learning

Make up a sentence or phrase to help you remember the names of the alkanes (this is known as a **mnemonic**); for example, Many Eat Proper Butter for methane, ethane, propane and butane.

The same prefixes are used to show the number of carbon atoms in most other homologous series so you just have to learn them once!

QUESTIONS

1   Look at the table which shows the alkane series and write down the formulae for

   a) propane

   b) pentane

   c) heptane.

2   Draw structures for ethane, butane, hexane and octane.

3   What is the connection between the number of carbon atoms and the number of hydrogen atoms in each alkane molecule?

Organic compounds

Crude oil was made from organic (living) material so the compounds obtained from crude oil are often called **organic compounds**. Chemists have made quite a number of carbon compounds that are not found in nature, but these are all still referred to as organic compounds.

Natural gas

Natural gas is a mixture, and the compounds present in the mixture vary, depending on where in the world the gas comes from. Usually, natural gas is around 70–90% methane, 5–15% ethane and 3% propane plus a range of other hydrocarbons and a lot of smelly sulphur compounds that have to be removed before the gas can be sold as a fuel. Natural gas also contains enough helium for it to be a main source of the element. These days the ethane and propane are **cracked** to make ethene and propene, which are both **feedstocks** for the plastics industry. Methane is the main component of the gas we use for cooking and heating and is also an important source of hydrogen. Hydrogen is a **primary feedstock** for the chemical industry. It is used:

- via the **Haber Process** to make fertilisers
- in oil refineries for **hydrocracking**
- to make margarine
- in hydrogen-powered vehicles.

Carbon compounds found in crude oil

Hydrocarbons derived from crude oil and natural gas

One of the most important groups of compounds made from crude oil is the **alkenes**. Each member of this homologous series contains at least one carbon-to-carbon double covalent bond. They are named in the same way as the alkanes, except that each name ends in the letters –ene to show that the compound is an alkene.

Number of carbon atoms in each molecule	Prefix	Name of alkene	What the molecule looks like (called the structure of the molecule)	Formula
two C atoms	eth	ethene	H–C=C–H with H H below	C_2H_4
three C atoms	prop	propene		C_3H_6
four C atoms	but	butene	H–C–C–C=C structure	
five C atoms	pent	pentene		
six C atoms	hex	hexene		C_6H_{12}
seven C atoms	hept	heptene	H–C–C–C–C–C–C=C structure	
eight C atoms	oct	octene		C_8H_{16}

The alkene series

QUESTIONS

1 Why is there not a compound called 'methene'?

2 Look at the table which shows the alkene series and write down the formulae for

   a) butene

   b) pentene

   c) heptene.

3 Draw structures for propene, pentene, hexene and octene.

4 What is the connection between the number of carbon atoms and the number of hydrogen atoms in each alkene molecule?

Plastics and polymers

Alkenes are the original feedstock for the plastics (polymer) industry. Any organic molecule that contains a carbon-to-carbon double bond can join up with other molecules of the same type to form very big molecules. The small alkene molecules are called **monomers** (mono = one, mer = unit) and the big molecules, made when thousands of these monomers join together, are called polymers (poly = many). ⟹

Polythene

This is the most widely used plastic in the world (around 80 million tonnes are made each year) and is the polymer used to make supermarket plastic bags. Polythene is its trade name but its chemical name is poly(ethene) and it is made from the monomer ethene. Polythene (also known in the plastics industry as polyethylene) has been known since the 1930s and there are now around seven different types of polythene, each designed for a different use. Two of these are:

- High Density Polyethylene (HDPE) – used for milk containers, shampoo bottles and margarine tubs.

- Low Density Polyethylene (LDPE) – used in squeezable bottles and frozen food bags.

Polystyrene

This is probably the second most widely used plastic in the world. It appears in our lives in many different disguises: as packaging for fruit and fragile items, and as disposable cups.

These three do not look the same, but they are all made of polystyrene

When polymerised with another hydrocarbon called butadiene, polystyrene makes poly(styrene-butadiene-styrene) or SBS, which is used to make the soles of your shoes and the treads on car tyres.

Carbon compounds in everyday life

Most of the things that you touch, wear and walk on each day are made from (or contain) some type of polymer. Mobile phone cases, computer housings, cars, carpets, the varnish on wood – all these are made from carefully designed polymers. If we carry on burning fossil fuels as we are at the moment, the raw material for all these plastics will literally go up in smoke. Look around you and imagine what would happen if all the polymers suddenly vanished. Plastics make our lives comfortable; perhaps this is another reason, other than global warming, for not burning fossil fuels.

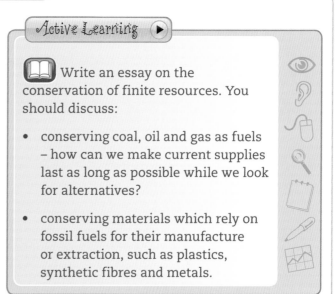

Active Learning ▶

📖 Write an essay on the conservation of finite resources. You should discuss:

- conserving coal, oil and gas as fuels – how can we make current supplies last as long as possible while we look for alternatives?

- conserving materials which rely on fossil fuels for their manufacture or extraction, such as plastics, synthetic fibres and metals.

GLOSSARY

Addition polymerisation many small molecules (monomers) join together to form one large molecule (a polymer) and nothing else

Condensation polymerisation many small molecules (monomers) join together to form one large molecule (a polymer) with another small molecule such as water formed at the same time

Cracked large hydrocarbon molecules (usually alkanes) are broken up to make a mixture of smaller ones (usually alkanes and alkenes)

Feedstock a processed chemical from which other chemicals are made

Fraction a mixture of hydrocarbons with similar boiling points obtained by fractional distillation of crude oil

Fractional distillation the technique used to separate mixtures which depends on the mixed substances having different boiling points

Haber Process the industrial production of ammonia (NH_3) from nitrogen and hydrogen using iron as a catalyst

Homologous series a group of compounds which all have the same general formula and similar chemical properties

Hydrocarbon a compound that contains the elements hydrogen and carbon only

Hydrocracking the process of cracking large hydrocarbon molecules in the presence of excess hydrogen to produce more alkanes rather than alkenes

Monomer small molecules which can join together to form very large molecules (polymers) by a process called polymerisation

Organic related to, or the remains of, living matter

Porous word used to describe a solid which has holes in its surface, and throughout the body of the material, which can hold liquids and/or gases

Prehistoric a period before written history began

Sedimentary a soft rock made by layers of sediment (sand, silt or mud, etc) sinking into the ground and being compressed over millions of years

Volatile a substance is volatile if it has a low boiling point and is easily evaporated (turned into a vapour)

MATERIALS
Chemical changes

3

Metals and the reactivity series

Level 3   What came before?

 SCN 3-19b

I have helped to design and carry out practical activities to develop my understanding of chemical reactions involving the Earth's materials. I can explain how we apply knowledge of these reactions in practical ways.

Level 4   What is this chapter about?

 SCN 4-19b

Having carried out a range of experiments using different chemicals, I can place metals in an order of reactivity, and relate my findings to their everyday uses.

 SCN 4-04b

Through investigation, I can explain the formation of fossil fuels and contribute to discussions on the responsible use and conservation of finite resources.

Metals and the reactivity series

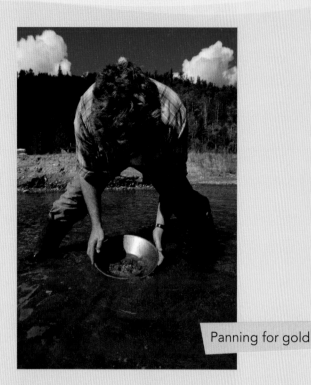

Panning for gold

Panning for gold

Gold has been treasured for centuries. Egyptian tombs have been opened to reveal beautiful gold jewellery, and shipwrecks have been explored in the hope of finding a treasure chest filled with gold. Today, gold continues to be highly valued and it is still used to make jewellery and ornaments. More recently it has been used to make electronic devices which rely on gold's ability to conduct electricity and resist corrosion.

It should come as no surprise that gold continues to be mined and is still considered to be one of the most valuable metals on the planet. And yet if gold were a more reactive metal, the story would be very different. One of the reasons that gold has been used for thousands of years is because it is a very unreactive metal; it is so unreactive that it can be found in the earth, rivers and streams. Even today people pan for gold in the rivers of Scotland in places such as Wanlockhead where the World Gold Panning Championships were held in 1992.

Most other metals are too reactive to exist on their own as elements. Usually they are found as compounds known as **ores** from which the pure metal can be extracted. Once the pure metal is left in the air, it is not long before it starts to react with the water and oxygen in the air. For example, pure copper is a bright shiny brown metal. After a few years it starts to react to form a green compound which is known as copper verdigris. This can be seen on the domes of old buildings such as the Mitchell Library in Glasgow. Reactive metals such as potassium only have to be exposed to air for a few seconds before they start to react and form a compound.

When potassium is cut, the surface is shiny

A new copper roof

After a very short time, the cut surface of the potassium has become tarnished after reacting with the air

In this chapter you will find out about metal reactivity and how we can create an order of reactivity for the metals we are familiar with from the Periodic Table.

The copper roof of Glasgow's Mitchell Library has become green over time

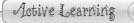

Active Learning

1 📖 Produce a presentation which shows the modern day uses of gold, the cost of gold, where it is mined and other interesting facts.

2 Find out about gold mining in Wanlockhead, Scotland.

The reactivity series of metals

Potassium
Sodium
Lithium
Calcium
Magnesium
Aluminium
Zinc
Iron
Tin
Lead
Copper
Mercury
Silver
Gold

The list of metals shown here displays the order of reactivity for the metals we use in the school chemistry laboratory. This list was created by observing how reactive metals are when reacted with water, acid or oxygen and is known as the **reactivity series**.

Reacting with water

The most reactive metals in the Periodic Table are so reactive that they even react with cold water. The Alkali Metals from Group 1 react spectacularly when added to a trough of water, with some of them producing brightly coloured flames. By reacting metals with water, we can put them in an order of reactivity. Potassium, sodium, lithium and calcium all react with cold water. Potassium reacts violently, bursting into flames. Sodium and lithium react vigorously, producing a gas. Calcium reacts a little slower than lithium and also produces a gas. Hopefully your teacher will demonstrate the reaction of the Alkali Metals with water and allow you to test the reaction of other metals with water.

Potassium reacting with water

What is produced when metals react with water?

Some metals react quickly with water to produce hydrogen gas and an alkali. This can be shown as a word equation:

sodium + water → sodium hydroxide + hydrogen

or as a chemical equation showing formulae:

$2Na(s) + 2H_2O(l) \rightarrow 2NaOH(aq) + H_2(g)$

Note:

In this equation, the **state** of each substance is indicated using a **state symbol**. There are four state symbols which you should learn because they are often used in equations to provide extra information:

- (s) means solid

- (l) means liquid

- (g) means gas

- (aq) means aqueous – dissolved in water.

Other metals react too slowly with water or do not react at all. For these metals, acid can be used to work out the order of reactivity.

QUESTIONS

1 Explain why the Group 1 metals are known as the 'Alkali Metals'.

2 How could you show that calcium reacting with water makes:

   a) calcium hydroxide

   b) hydrogen gas?

3 Write (a) word equations and (b) chemical equations showing formulae for the following metals reacting with water:

   i) potassium

   ii) lithium.

4 a) How are the Alkali Metals stored?

   b) Why are they stored this way?

5 What happens to the reactivity of the Group 1 metals as you go down the Group?

Active Learning ▶

1 Carry out an experiment to prove that calcium reacts with water to produce an alkali and hydrogen gas.

2 Make your own lime water. Find out about lime water and what it is used to test for. You can make lime water by following the steps below:

   a) React some calcium with water.

   b) Filter the remains.

   c) Carefully blow into the solution and observe what happens.

   d) Explain your findings.

Reacting with acid

Reacting metals with acid helps us come up with an order of reactivity for the remaining metals which do not react with water.

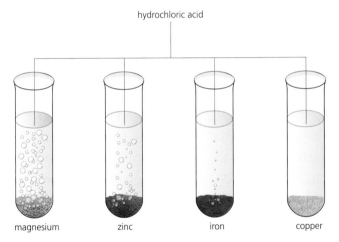

hydrochloric acid

magnesium   zinc   iron   copper

Carrying out these simple reactions by adding a spatula full of the metal powder to some dilute hydrochloric acid allows us to come up with the order as:

magnesium > zinc > iron
(> means 'is more reactive than')

Copper, mercury, silver and gold do not react with dilute acid.

What is produced when a metal reacts with an acid?

If you carry out this experiment in the lab, you will notice that the reactive metals all produce a gas. If you collect this gas and place a lit splint in the gas, it pops showing that it is hydrogen. The reaction also produces another product which is known as a salt.

For example, when magnesium reacts with hydrochloric acid the products are magnesium chloride (the salt) and hydrogen. This can be shown as a word equation:

magnesium + hydrochloric → magnesium + hydrogen
$\qquad$ acid $\qquad$ chloride

or as a chemical equation showing formulae:

$$Mg(s) + 2HCl(aq) \rightarrow MgCl_2(aq) + H_2(g)$$

The lack of reactivity of gold was used during the Californian gold rush to test if a metal really was gold. This test became known as 'the acid test'. Miners trying to sell their 'gold' to gold merchants would have to watch nervously as the merchant placed a few drops of nitric acid onto the gold and waited for signs of reaction. If there was no fizzing, the gold had passed the acid test!

Nitric Acid

QUESTIONS

1 Write word equations for the reactions of the following metals with hydrochloric acid:

   a) zinc   b) iron   c) tin.

2 How could you show that the hydrochloric acid is reacting (being used up) when metals react with acid?

3 Zinc sulphate is a salt which can be used as a medicine, for killing moss and as a preservative. What do you think would be reacted with zinc to make zinc sulphate?

Active Learning ▶

1 Carry out experiments to find the order of reactivity of copper, iron, magnesium, tin and zinc. For the most reactive metal, test the gas produced. You could test for oxygen, hydrogen and carbon dioxide.

2 Find out about the Californian gold rush or the Scottish gold rush in the nineteenth century.

3 Find out how gold can be made to react with an acid and how a famous chemist (Niels Bohr) used this to stop his gold Nobel Prize medal from being stolen.

Reacting with oxygen

The reactivity of metals can also be studied by observing the reaction of the metal with oxygen. Very reactive metals, such as the Alkali Metals, react with the oxygen in the air within a few seconds. Other metals can be made to react quickly with oxygen by heating them in the air. For example, you will be familiar with the bright glow that is seen when magnesium is held in a Bunsen flame. This is the reaction of magnesium with oxygen.

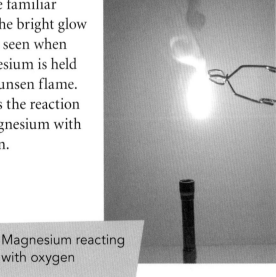
Magnesium reacting with oxygen

For the unreactive metals, we have to roast the metals in pure oxygen gas to encourage them to react.

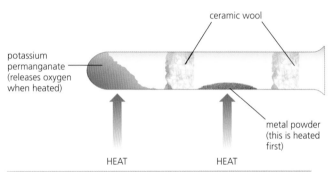

potassium permanganate (releases oxygen when heated)

ceramic wool

metal powder (this is heated first)

HEAT   HEAT

Metals can be heated in oxygen to find out how reactive they are

The apparatus shown above can be used to study the reactivity of the metals from magnesium to copper. Potassium permanganate has the formula $KMnO_4$ so it is very rich in oxygen. Heating it releases oxygen which is passed over the hot metal causing it to glow; the brighter the glow, the more reactive the metal. The product of this reaction is the metal oxide. For example:

$$copper + oxygen \rightarrow copper\ (II)\ oxide$$

$$2Cu(s) + O_2(g) \rightarrow 2CuO(s)$$

Mercury, silver and gold are so unreactive that it is very difficult to get them to react with oxygen.

Metal	Reaction with		
	Oxygen	Water	Diluted acid
potassium	metal + oxygen ↓ metal oxide	metal + water ↓ metal hydroxide + hydrogen	metal + acid ↓ salt + hydrogen
sodium			
lithium			
calcium			
magnesium			
aluminium			
zinc			
iron			
tin			
lead		no reaction	
copper			
mercury			no reaction
silver	no reaction		
gold			

Metals glow brightly as they react with oxygen

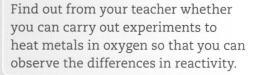

Active Learning ▶

Find out from your teacher whether you can carry out experiments to heat metals in oxygen so that you can observe the differences in reactivity.

Displacement

Another method used to place the metals in an order of reactivity is a reaction known as **displacement**. If a more reactive metal is added to a compound of a less reactive metal, a reaction takes place. For example, if aluminium is added to iron (III) oxide and heated, a vigorous reaction takes place causing molten iron to form.

aluminium + iron (III) → aluminium + iron
oxide   oxide

$$2Al(s) + Fe_2O_3(s) \rightarrow Al_2O_3(s) + 2Fe(l)$$

QUESTIONS

1 Predict what would be seen if a strip of magnesium was heated in pure oxygen.

2 Write (a) a word equation and (b) a chemical equation showing formulae for the reaction of magnesium with oxygen.

3 Sparklers contain iron filings and a compound which releases oxygen when heated. Name one of the compounds formed when a sparkler burns.

The reactivity series of metals

This is known as a **thermite** reaction. The reaction is highly **exothermic** and so much heat is produced that the iron formed is actually molten. It can be used as a source of molten iron to repair railway tracks and has also been used by the military as thermite bombs.

A thermite reaction

You can also observe a displacement reaction if you leave an iron nail in a solution of copper (II) sulphate. After a few minutes copper metal starts to form around the iron nail.

iron + copper (II) → iron (II) + copper
      sulphate   sulphate

$$Fe(s) + CuSO_4(aq) \rightarrow FeSO_4(aq) + Cu(s)$$

In this displacement reaction, copper metal can be seen forming on the iron nail

Displacement reactions can help us decide which metal is more reactive. In the above example we can see that the iron has 'displaced' the copper. This shows us that iron is more reactive than

copper. If the experiment is repeated by placing a piece of copper in a solution of iron (II) sulphate, no reaction takes place as the copper is not reactive enough to displace the iron.

copper + iron (II) sulphate → no reaction

You can think of displacement as being like a competition. The more reactive metal will always win, leaving the less reactive metal on its own.

The reactions of metals with water, acid and oxygen together with displacement reactions all provide evidence for the order of reactivity of metals given on page 34.

QUESTIONS

1 Predict whether the following would react:

  a) lithium + sodium oxide

  b) copper + mercury (II) chloride

  c) iron + magnesium oxide

  d) magnesium + zinc (II) sulphate.

2 All acids contain hydrogen. When a metal reacts with acid, hydrogen is released. This can be thought of as a displacement reaction. Using your knowledge of the reactions of metals with acids, where would you place hydrogen in the reactivity series?

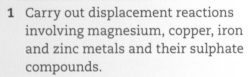

1 Carry out displacement reactions involving magnesium, copper, iron and zinc metals and their sulphate compounds.

2 Find out two uses of displacement reactions in everyday life.

3 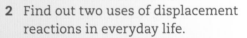 Create a poem, song or story to help you and your class remember the reactivity series.

Uses of metals

Think of the world without metals. Look around you and you will see many objects that are made of metal and many objects that contain metals. But did you know that metals are another **finite** resource and that because of this they must be used responsibly to conserve what we have?

Metals are so widely used because of their variety of chemical and physical properties, such as:

1 **Electrical conductivity** – all metals conduct electricity, but some conduct better than others.

2 **Thermal conductivity** – all metals conduct heat, although again, some better than others.

3 **Reactivity** – as you now know, different metals have different reactivities, from silver which is very unreactive and can be used as jewellery, to magnesium which is much more reactive and burns with an extremely bright flame. For this reason, magnesium is used in distress flares.

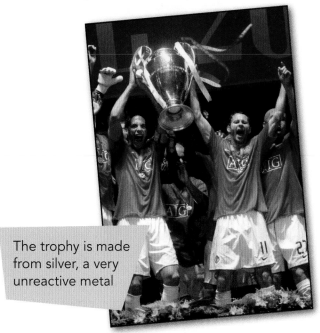

The trophy is made from silver, a very unreactive metal

4 **Malleability** – if a substance can be shaped by a hammer, for example, or rolled into sheets then it is said to be **malleable**. Most metals are malleable.

5 **Ductility** – metals can be stretched out to form wires. They are said to be **ductile**.

Active Learning ▶

1 Construct an electric circuit with a gap in it using a battery, a bulb or ammeter, two crocodile clips and three leads to test the conductivity of various metals when they are placed across the gap. Present your results in a table.

2 Attach a drawing pin to one end of a metal rod using wax or grease. Heat the other end of the metal with a Bunsen burner and time how long it takes for the drawing pin to fall off the metal rod when the wax or grease melts. Repeat this using rods made from different metals. The faster the drawing pin drops off, the higher the thermal conductivity of that metal. Present your results in a table.

3 Make lists of several examples of named metals being used in everyday life for reasons connected with their ability to conduct electricity or heat.

Alloys

When you hear the word **alloy** you may think of a fancy type of wheel on a car but there is a lot more to alloys than that.

An alloy is formed when a metal is first melted and then mixed with one or more other elements, which are usually other metals. Alloys are made to produce metals with the properties required to do a specific job. This means that there are a lot of different forms of alloys, all of which have specific properties for specific purposes.

Stainless steel, brass and solder are examples of alloys. Each has very different properties.

Stainless steel is an alloy of iron, carbon (a non-metal) and chromium. Stainless steel does not stain or corrode as easily as ordinary steel which is an alloy of iron and carbon only. Stainless steel has many uses because of its resistance to corrosion, from cutlery to constructions such as the Gateway Arch in St Louis.

Brass is an alloy of copper and zinc. It has many uses too, from decoration due to its bright gold-like appearance, to musical instruments because of its acoustic properties.

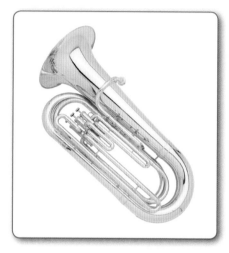

Solder is an alloy with a relatively low melting point. This makes it very useful in joining metallic surfaces together in electrical circuits or plumbing.

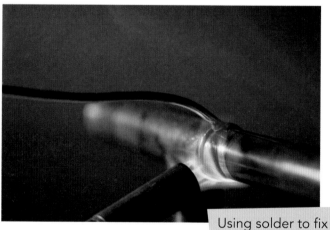

Using solder to fix a copper pipe

The Gateway Arch is made from stainless steel

Active Learning

1 Present the following list of metals in a table under the headings 'Element' and 'Alloy':

   gold, silver, bronze, solder, steel, calcium, iron, brass, zinc.

2 Coins are made from alloys. Find out which metals are used, and in what proportions, to make these British coins – 1p, 2p, 5p, 10p, 20p, 50p, £1 and £2.

3 Find out why some 1p coins are attracted to a magnet while others are not.

4 'Silver' coins used to be made from pure silver. Think of some reasons why this is no longer the case.

5 Manufacturers of sports cars are now putting magnesium alloy wheels on cars. Do some research to find the advantages and disadvantages of using magnesium alloys for wheels. Apart from magnesium, what else are these wheels made of?

Conservation and recycling of metals

Steel and aluminium are two of the most widely used metals in the UK and must therefore be produced in large quantities. Although in the UK the consumption of steel has dropped since the 1970s, aluminium use is still growing.

Twenty-four million tonnes of aluminium are produced each year in the world, with the largest producer of aluminium being Australia. Other producer countries include Jamaica, Brazil, Guinea, China and parts of Europe.

Metals, however, are finite and we cannot maintain this level of production forever. We must therefore look at ways of recycling metals.

Metals can be recycled indefinitely without losing any of their properties. They make up around 8% of the contents of the average household dustbin, yet only a very small percentage of this is recycled.

Aluminium

Aluminium is produced from bauxite, a clay-like ore that is rich in aluminium oxide. This aluminium ore has to be stripped of its oxygen. This is done by a process known as **electrolysis** because aluminium is a fairly reactive metal. This process uses large quantities of energy.

If 1 kg of aluminium is produced by recycling, up to 6 kg of bauxite, 4 kg of chemical products and 14 kWh of electricity are saved. This means that recycling one aluminium can saves enough energy to run a television for three hours!

Recycling aluminium requires only 5% of the energy and produces only 5% of the carbon dioxide emissions compared with production of aluminium from its ore. In addition, recycling reduces the waste going to landfill.

ALUMINIUM

Steel

Earlier we learned that steel is an alloy produced from iron which is also mined from an ore. The iron used to make steel is produced in the **blast furnace**.

If 1 tonne of steel is recycled, up to 1.5 tonnes of iron ore, 0.5 tonnes of coal and 75% of the energy needed to make iron from iron ore are saved. In addition, the amount of water pollution is reduced by 76% and the amount of waste put into the atmosphere is reduced by 86%.

Over 2.5 billion steel cans are recycled in the UK each year. That is a saving of 125 000 tonnes of solid waste every year – equivalent to the weight of 18 000 double decker buses!

But this is only 46% of the steel cans that are disposed of in Britain each year.

Other metals

All metals including nickel, copper, silver, gold, lead, brass and many more can be recycled. Given their recognised value, a smaller quantity of these metals is in circulation.

Active Learning

Recycling of metals is very important because they are a finite resource. Produce a presentation or a poster to promote recycling and to highlight why the recycling of metals is so important.

GLOSSARY

Alloy a mixture of a metal with another element, usually another metal

Blast furnace the industrial method used to extract iron from its ore

Displacement a reaction where a metal higher in the reactivity series reacts with a compound of a metal lower in the reactivity series; the reactive metal forms a compound and the unreactive metal is formed as a free element

Ductile the ability of a metal to be drawn out into wires

Electrolysis the separation of an ionic compound using electricity

Exothermic a process in which energy is released

Finite when a material or substance is running out and cannot be replaced

Malleable the ability of a metal to be rolled or beaten into thin sheets

Ore the state in which some metals are found in nature

Reactivity series a list of metals (and hydrogen) in order of reactivity

Thermite a mixture of a reactive metal and a metal compound which will react exothermically

FORCES, ELECTRICITY AND WAVES

Electricity

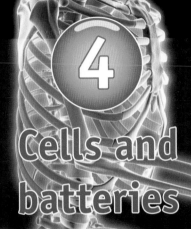

4
Cells and batteries

Level 3　What came before?

SCN 3-10a

I can help to design simple chemical cells and use them to investigate the factors which affect the voltage produced.

Level 4　What is this chapter about?

SCN 4-10a

Using experimental evidence, I can place metals in an electrochemical series and can use this information to make predictions about their use in chemical cells.

SCN 4-10b

Using a variety of sources, I have explored the latest developments in chemical cells technology and can evaluate their impact on society.

Cells and batteries

Batteries everywhere

How different would your life be without batteries? Think of all the gadgets that use batteries. There are thousands of uses, from mobile phones and iPods® to laptops, watches and electronic games.

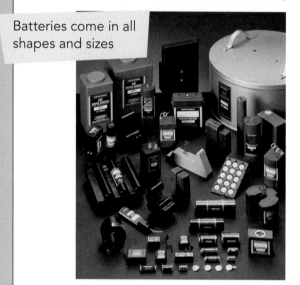

Batteries come in all shapes and sizes

Batteries have also helped to improve the quality of life of people who need to use hearing aids, electric wheelchairs and pacemakers. Yet, how often have you thought about how batteries actually work?

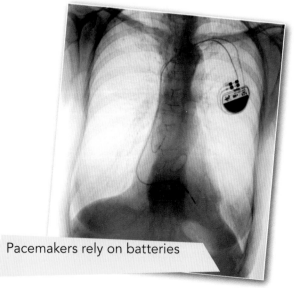

Pacemakers rely on batteries

In this chapter you will find out about batteries and their many uses.

Galvani and the twitching frog

Luigi Galvani was an Italian scientist who helped start the invention of the first battery. In the late 1700s, Galvani was experimenting with frogs when he observed that he was able to cause twitching in a dead frog's legs by touching exposed nerves with two different metals.

Luigi Galvani

Galvani was convinced that he had discovered a new form of electricity which was different from lightning and other forms of **static electricity**. He believed that this electricity was inside the frog's legs and that he had helped to guide it into the nerves to cause the frog's legs to twitch. →

Batteries everywhere

Another Italian scientist, Alessandro Volta, did not agree with Galvani's conclusions. Volta said that the electricity was created by the two metals being in contact with the moist frog. Volta was able to show that he could create electricity by using two different metals and a salt solution.

Alessandro Volta

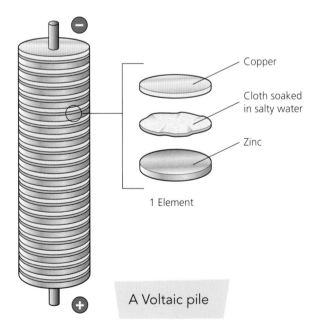

A Voltaic pile

Volta created the first battery by stacking zinc and copper discs together with paper soaked in salt solution between the metals. This became known as the **Voltaic pile**.

Copper

Cloth soaked in salty water

Zinc

1 Element

We can confirm Volta's experiments in the school laboratory by simply dipping two different metals into a beaker full of salty water. If we connect a meter to the two metals, we get a reading showing us that electricity is flowing!

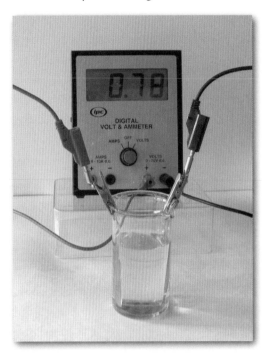

This arrangement of metals and salt solution to create electricity is known as a **chemical cell**. When two or more cells are joined together to make electricity, it is known as a battery. Nowadays, many chemical cells are often referred to as batteries.

Active Learning

1 Find out about Galvani and Volta. Create a poster to show your findings.

2 Think of all the things which use batteries. Write a short story entitled 'When all the batteries ran out'.

3 Make a Voltaic pile.

4 List as many different battery types as you can. Why do we have so many different batteries?

Chemical cells: how do they work?

One of the great advantages of cells over mains electricity is that they are portable. They are a convenient source of electricity that can be used anywhere in the world, from the remotest spot in the Amazonian rainforest to power a digital camera to busy cities to power a mobile phone. We study cells in chemistry because they involve a chemical reaction in which chemical energy is changed into electrical energy. Rechargeable batteries allow us to reverse this reaction so that electrical energy is changed to chemical energy.

Battery being used

Chemical energy ⇄ **Electrical energy**

Battery being charged

Simple cells are made using two different **electrodes** (such as copper and zinc) and a conducting solution or paste which contains charged particles known as **ions**. In the Voltaic pile, the conducting solution is simply salty water. The conducting solution is known as the **electrolyte**. When the two electrodes are dipped in the electrolyte, **electrons** flow from one electrode to the other. This flow of electrons is known as an **electric current**.

The electrolyte is essential. If the two metals are connected together without the electrolyte, no electricity is produced.

Acid or alkali?

The electrolyte in a battery can be seen when a battery is cut open or left to 'leak'. The electrolyte is usually quite corrosive as it is either an acid or an alkali. You will often see this referred to on the packaging for batteries.

An alkaline battery

The electrolyte can be seen when a battery is leaking

Voltage

Cells and batteries 'push' electrons around circuits. The energy in this push is known as **voltage**. Different appliances use cells or batteries of different voltages. For example, a 3-volt battery is commonly used in watches, whereas a 9-volt battery is used in a household smoke alarm.

Batteries come in a range of different voltages

Most cars use a battery: starting the engine and working the lights, heater, windscreen wipers, CD player and so on requires a supply of electricity. The battery found in a car produces 12 volts from six 2-volt cells connected **in series**, and it is an unusual battery for two reasons. First, the electrodes in each cell are both made from the same metal – lead. Second, the battery can be recharged. When the car moves, an electric current is sent through the battery causing it to charge. The electrolyte in a car battery is a solution of sulphuric acid, so the battery is called a lead–acid battery.

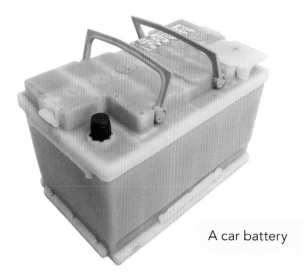

A car battery

Perhaps the most fun batteries are those made from fruit! If you insert two different metals into a piece of fruit, you can produce a small current. The current is enough to power a small bulb or clock. How does it work? Most fruit batteries are acid batteries. If you have ever squeezed a lemon or orange onto a small cut on your finger, you will know that it stings! These fruits contain citric acid which acts as the electrolyte in the same way that salt water acts as the electrolyte in the Voltaic pile. Inserting two metals into the fruit allows a current to flow between the two metals.

QUESTIONS

1 State the advantages and disadvantages of batteries compared to mains electricity.

2 What is an electrolyte?

3 Why do you think most batteries 'run out' and have to be thrown away?

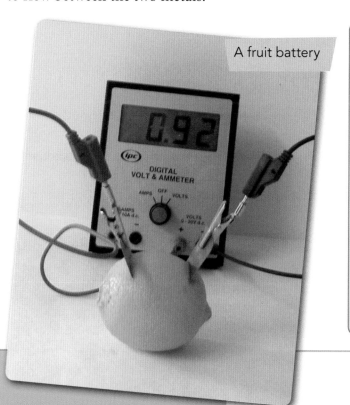

A fruit battery

Active Learning ▶

1 Build some fruit cells using zinc and copper strips, connecting wires, crocodile clips and a voltmeter. Use different fruits and find out which one produces the highest voltage.

2 Find out the names of the acid and alkali electrolytes used in common batteries.

3 Compare two cell types to find out which one is best value for money. You will have to design an experiment which allows you to test how long each cell can power an electrical device (e.g. a bulb).

Current, voltage and the electrochemical series

When the apparatus shown on page 45 is connected using zinc and copper, a current flows from zinc to copper. If the zinc is replaced by magnesium, the current still flows towards copper, but the voltage is much higher. If the zinc is replaced by iron, the current still flows towards copper, but the voltage is much lower! The results from this experiment are shown in the table on the right.

Metals connected together	Direction of current flow	Voltage (V)
zinc and copper	zinc to copper	1.0
magnesium and copper	magnesium to copper	2.1
iron and copper	iron to copper	0.7

If iron is replaced by copper (leaving two copper electrodes), the reading on the voltmeter is zero. If the new copper one is replaced by silver or gold, a reading is obtained on the meter but it is a negative number! By carrying out these experiments, a league table of metals can be produced:

Magnesium
Zinc
Iron
Copper
Silver or gold

By carrying out the same experiment with lots of different metals, a larger league table known as the **electrochemical series** (ECS) is produced (this is not the same as the reactivity series but it is very similar):

Lithium
Potassium
Calcium
Sodium
Magnesium
Aluminium
Zinc
Iron
Nickel
Tin
Lead
Copper
Silver
Mercury
Gold

You can use the electrochemical series to make statements about the voltage and direction of current flow when two metals are used to make a cell.

Voltage: The bigger the gap in the ECS, the bigger the voltage.

Connecting magnesium to copper produces a much larger voltage than connecting iron to copper because the gap in the ECS is bigger between magnesium and copper than the gap between iron and copper.

Current: Current flows from high to low.

If magnesium is connected to copper, the current will flow from magnesium to copper. If copper is connected to gold, the current will flow from copper to gold.

QUESTIONS

1   State the direction of current flow when the following pairs of metals are connected:

a) lead and iron

b) zinc and silver

c) nickel and aluminium.

2   Which pair of metals from Question 1 would produce the highest voltage?

Active Learning

Carry out experiments with aluminium, copper, iron, magnesium, tin and zinc to create your own electrochemical series. Show that 'current flows from high to low' and 'the bigger the gap, the bigger the voltage' hold true for these six metals.

Oxidation and reduction

In the magnesium–copper cell, the current flows from magnesium to copper. Let us look at why this happens.

When a metal is placed in an electrolyte, the metal atoms start to form ions. Atoms contain equal numbers of protons and electrons and so are neutral – you learned this in Chapter 1. Metal atoms form ions by losing electrons, meaning that the ions formed have more protons than electrons and so are positively charged. In the case of magnesium, this can be shown by an equation:

$$Mg(s) \rightarrow Mg^{2+}(aq) + 2e^-$$

This is known as an **ion–electron equation**. It shows the magnesium atom losing two electrons to form a magnesium ion. The fact that the ion has two more protons than electrons is shown by the 'two positive' (2+) charge.

If copper is placed in an electrolyte, it also starts to form copper ions:

$$Cu(s) \rightarrow Cu^{2+}(aq) + 2e^-$$

These equations show that both metals are losing electrons – in both cases they are losing two electrons. However, metals are all different. Some metals, like magnesium, lose electrons very easily. Other metals, like copper, do not lose electrons as easily. Furthermore, some metal atoms lose two electrons when forming ions whereas some may only lose one and others may lose three or even four. The number of electrons lost is the number found in the outer energy level – the one furthest from the nucleus. (Remember that you learned that electrons are found moving around the nucleus of an atom in energy levels in Chapter 1.)

So if magnesium is connected to copper, magnesium atoms lose electrons and the electrons flow to copper. This can be shown by two ion–electron equations. First, magnesium atoms lose electrons:

$$Mg(s) \rightarrow Mg^{2+}(aq) + 2e^-$$

The process of losing electrons is known as **oxidation**.

The lost electrons flow through the meter to the copper. This causes another reaction to occur at the copper electrode where something gains these electrons. For example, you may see bubbles of gas forming on the copper if the electrolyte is salty water. These will be bubbles of hydrogen produced when hydrogen ions in water gain electrons:

$$2H^+(aq) + 2e^- \rightarrow H_2(g)$$

The process of gaining electrons is known as **reduction**.

These two equations can be combined to show an overall **red**uction and **ox**idation equation. This is known as a **redox** equation:

$$Mg(s) + 2H^+(aq) \rightarrow Mg^{2+}(aq) + H_2(g)$$

You will see that the two electrons from each separate ion–electron equation are missing. That is because they cancel out: the two electrons lost by the magnesium atom are gained by the hydrogen ions.

QUESTIONS

1 Using the examples shown above, write oxidation equations for the following:

 a) a sodium atom losing one electron

 b) a zinc atom losing two electrons

 c) an aluminium atom losing three electrons.

2 Write reduction equations for the following:

 a) a nickel 2+ ion gaining two electrons

 b) a gold 1+ ion gaining one electron

 c) a lead 2+ ion gaining two electrons.

Oxidation and reduction

In this chapter we have looked at creating cells by connecting two different metals together that are dipped in an electrolyte. There are other methods of connecting metals together which can be used to find out about current and voltage. Investigate the two methods below for making cells.

The sandwich cell

This consists of two different metals and some filter paper soaked in an electrolyte.

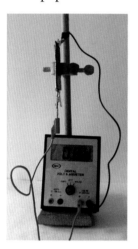
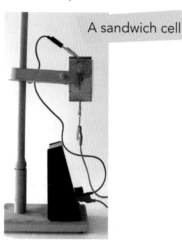

A sandwich cell

Sandwich cells are easy to set up. Investigate what happens to the voltage if you let the filter paper dry out.

Two half cells

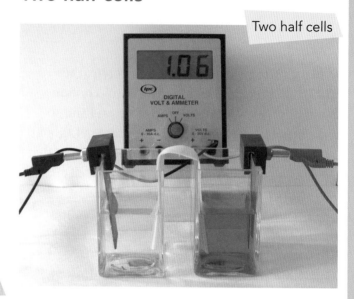

Two half cells

This method involves connecting two different metals in solutions of their own ions. The two ionic solutions (electrolytes) are connected by a piece of filter paper soaked in salt solution. This is known as the **ion bridge**. If you build this cell you can find out what happens when you remove the ion bridge. The ion bridge completes the circuit by allowing ions to flow between the two beakers.

QUESTIONS

Write the ion–electron equations for the zinc–copper cell shown.

New technology

Cell technology has developed at a very fast pace over the last 40 years. As consumers demanded that electronic devices were smaller, more lightweight and ran for longer, cells had to become more efficient. We take for granted devices like mobile phones which run on very small lithium ion batteries that can stay charged for several days. Yet, this is a quite recent invention. It took many years of research to create the cell technology that has led to the lightweight, rapidly rechargeable, long-life and safe cells that we use today.

New technology

Scientists and engineers continue to work together to create cells that can keep up with the demands of new technology. Cells that power cars and buses have started to make electric transport a reality. Hybrid cars have become much more common in the UK. These make use of traditional petrol or diesel engines, but they also have cells which can store and release energy for the car to use.

A hybrid car

Cell technology is changing rapidly. Sony recently announced that they had developed a bio-cell which created electricity using sugar and enzymes. The cell is still in development but it looks likely to be an exciting addition to the world of batteries.

Active Learning ▶

1 Find out about lithium polymer batteries and why they are used in so many electronic devices.

2 Find out about hybrid cars and the battery technology that helps them work.

3 📖 Write a newspaper article on the Sony bio-cell. Find out how far the research has progressed. Are we likely to find them in the shops soon?

The battery problem

What do you do with cells and batteries once they have stopped working? Many people simply throw them into normal waste bins. Did you know that this can seriously affect the environment? Cells and batteries contain many chemicals such as cadmium, lead and mercury which can cause harm to us if they get into our food supply or drinking water. In addition, throwing cells away is such a waste. They contain many valuable metals which are a finite resource. As a result, chemical cells should not be put in normal waste. Instead, they should be recycled at special battery recycling stations. These have become more popular since the EU Battery Directive forced shops which sell batteries to offer customers a place to recycle them.

A battery recycling box

Household Battery
Recycling

(Alkaline, Nickel Cadmium,
Lithium Ion, AA, AAA, C, D etc)

The battery problem

Batteries should not be disposed of with normal household waste

Compared to other European countries, the UK has been very poor at recycling batteries. Hopefully the new recycling stations will help us become much better at protecting our environment and reducing our waste.

 Active Learning

1 Find out about battery recycling in your local area.

2 Do a survey on battery disposal in your class. How could you encourage more people to recycle batteries?

3 How are batteries recycled? Find out about the battery recycling plant in Golspie and how the batteries are recycled.

4 Many countries have expressed concern about rich nations dumping toxic battery waste in poorer countries. Find out if this is happening and who it affects.

GLOSSARY

Electrochemical series a list of chemicals, mostly metals, used to predict the current and voltage produced when two of the chemicals are connected together in a chemical cell

Electrode an electrical conductor dipped into an electrolyte

Electrolyte a solution containing ions

Electron a negatively charged particle found in all atoms

In series components in a circuit connected in a single path

Ion a charged particle

Oxidation a reaction in which electrons are lost

Redox a reaction in which reduction and oxidation take place

Reduction a reaction in which electrons are gained

Static electricity charge picked up by an object which cannot conduct a current

MATERIALS
Chemical changes

5
Thermodynamics

Level 3 — What came before?

 SCN 3-19a

Through experimentation, I can identify indicators of chemical reactions having occurred. I can describe ways of controlling the rate of reactions and can relate my findings to the world around me.

Level 4 — What is this chapter about?

 SCN 4-19a

I can collect and analyse experimental data on chemical reactions that result in an obvious change in energy. I can apply my findings to explain the significance of the energy changes associated with chemical reactions.

Thermodynamics

Thermodynamics? Sounds complicated ...

Put simply, every chemical reaction involves an energy change. When chemical reactions take place, existing chemical bonds must be broken and new chemical bonds must be made. Energy must be used to break the bonds in the reactants but energy is released when bonds are formed in the products. When a reaction is finished:

- either more energy will have been used in breaking the old bonds than in forming the new ones, so overall energy has been taken in by the reaction, or

- more energy will have been released on forming the new ones than was used to break the old ones, and overall the reaction has given out energy.

This chapter is going to examine some of the exciting energy changes that take place in chemical reactions. **Thermodynamics** is the study of energy changes and we are going to look at what happens when energy is either given out or taken in by a chemical reaction.

Exothermic reactions

An **exothermic** reaction is one in which energy is released. This is often indicated by a temperature rise caused by the release of heat. However, energy could also be released during a chemical reaction in the form of sound or light. The most exciting chemical reactions will probably have all three going on!

Cannon fire demonstration

This is a great example of an exothermic reaction. A little potassium permanganate powder is sprinkled into a crucible containing a burning

mixture of ethanol and hydrogen peroxide. What follows is a stunning display of an exothermic reaction. While the flame is initially small and blue, indicating that it is burning very cleanly, the flames become noticeably larger and more purple. The reaction is very noisy too!

How does it work?

Potassium permanganate is an **oxidising agent**.

The symbol for an oxidising agent that you might see on the side of bottles of chemicals

Normally, hydrogen peroxide **decomposes** very slowly in daylight to form water and oxygen.

hydrogen peroxide → water + oxygen

$$2H_2O_2 \rightarrow 2H_2O + O_2$$

Potassium permanganate speeds this process up.

potassium permanganate + hydrogen peroxide → manganese dioxide + water + oxygen + potassium hydroxide

$$2KMnO_4 \quad + \quad 3H_2O_2 \quad \rightarrow \quad 2MnO_2 \quad + 2H_2O + \quad 3O_2 \quad + \quad 2KOH$$

Far more oxygen is produced with the potassium permanganate present, causing both the flame to grow and the 'cannon' sound to be produced.

Everyday exothermic reactions

Many exothermic reactions occur around us in everyday life. Whenever a fuel burns in a combustion reaction, energy is released. Whether it is a match, a candle, some ethanol or a bonfire, both heat energy and light energy are given out.

Exothermic reactions are not always so obvious. Neutralisation is another example of an exothermic reaction.

acid + alkali → salt + water

Active Learning

You have learned previously about neutralisation reactions and used an indicator to find out when they were complete. How can you show that the reaction is exothermic?

Measure out 25 cm³ of an acid solution into a beaker (or polystyrene cup) and take its temperature. Do the same with an alkali solution. If the temperatures are not the same, calculate their average temperature. Now pour one solution into the other and stir the mixture with a thermometer. What happens? Did other groups get the same result?

QUESTIONS

1   What does exothermic mean?

2   In the cannon fire demonstration:

  a) What do you think caused the flame to change colour?

  b) Potassium permanganate speeds up the reaction, but it does not act as a catalyst. Why is it **not** being called a catalyst for this reaction?

  c) Hydrogen peroxide is weakly acidic. What pH do you think hydrogen peroxide would be after it decomposes naturally?

  d) Why would the pH of the reaction mixture after the cannon fire demonstration be different? Suggest a new pH value.

The bomb calorimeter

The packaging of food contains important information about its contents. People who are watching their weight are often said to be 'counting the calories', but where do these values come from? Nowadays we measure energy in joules (J) or kilojoules (kJ) but in the nineteenth century calories (cal) were devised as a way of measuring energy and these are still commonly used when we are referring to food energy.

One calorie is defined as the energy required to raise the temperature of 1 cm³ of water by 1 °C. One calorie is approximately 4.2 joules. Since food contains a lot of energy, it is more common to see the values quoted in kilojoules (kJ) or kilocalories (kcal).

Exothermic reactions

A piece of equipment called a bomb **calorimeter** can be used to measure how much heat energy is given out when a fuel (in this case, a food) is burned.

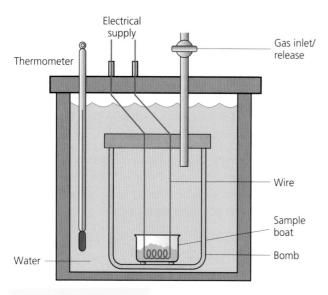

A bomb calorimeter

Electricity is used to ignite the fuel and the surrounding air is heated by the exothermic reaction. The hot air heats the water and the temperature rise can be measured with a thermometer.

QUESTIONS

1 Make a list of as many exothermic reactions that have happened today as you can.

2 Look at the information shown on the labels from three different drinks:

Dino-Fuel energy drink

Energy	Per serving (250 ml)
Energy	110 kcal
Total fat	0 g
Sugars	28 g
Protein	Less than 1 g

Freshly squeezed orange juice

Per serving (250 ml)	
Energy	344 kJ (82 kcal)
Total fat	<1 g
Sugars	26 g
Protein	<1 g

Bamboo Cola

Per serving (250 ml)	
Energy	586 kJ (140 kcal)
Total fat	0 g
Sugars	39 g
Protein	0 g

a) Which drink would give the most energy per 250 ml serving?

b) Bamboo Cola is sold in a 750 ml bottle. How much energy would your body get if you drank the whole bottle?

c) The Dino-Fuel energy drink label shows the energy in kcal. How much energy in kJ would one serving of Dino-Fuel contain? (1 kcal = 4.2 kJ)

d) Draw a bar graph comparing the energy values for each of the three drinks.

Active Learning

Ask your teacher if you can try to measure roughly how much energy we get from different foods. A sample of food can be weighed on a balance and then heated till it catches light in a Bunsen flame using a **deflagrating spoon**. The burning food can be held under a boiling tube of water and the temperature rise recorded.

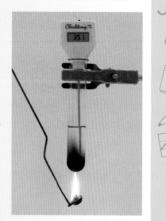

What measurements would you need to make to ensure that this was a fair experiment? How will you present your results?

Endothermic reactions

An **endothermic** reaction is one in which energy is taken in. This will often be shown by a drop in temperature. Endothermic reactions are less common in everyday life than exothermic reactions but still play important roles. Chemical cold packs used to treat bumps and sprains rely on an endothermic reaction to cool down the painful area. When the cold pack is squeezed, the inner bag bursts and the chemicals mix. The result is an endothermic reaction that cools the pack down and it can be used to stop or reduce swelling.

Another example of an important endothermic reaction is **photosynthesis**, the process that plants use to make food. Carbon dioxide and water react together in the plant to form glucose and oxygen:

$$6CO_2 + 6H_2O \rightarrow C_6H_{12}O_6 + 6O_2$$

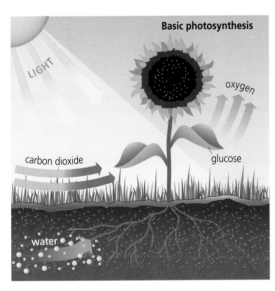

Basic photosynthesis

LIGHT

oxygen

carbon dioxide

glucose

water

This process would not be possible without sunlight. The plant must absorb 15 kJ of light energy to produce 1 g of glucose.

Active Learning ▶

Ask your teacher if you can make endothermic sherbet! Dissolve some citric acid in water and take the temperature of the solution. Add some sodium hydrogencarbonate powder and be prepared for lots of fizzing and a drop in temperature.

A great demonstration of an endothermic reaction involves mixing barium hydroxide octahydrate ($Ba(OH)_2.8H_2O$) with ammonium chloride (NH_4Cl). The two powders are placed in a beaker and stirred with the probe of a digital thermometer. As they are mixed, the powders turn slushy and the temperature starts to drop dramatically. From starting at room temperature, the reaction mixture can drop to a temperature of around −30 °C!

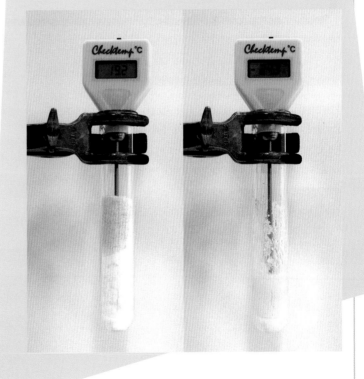

Endothermic reactions

QUESTIONS

1 What does endothermic mean?

2 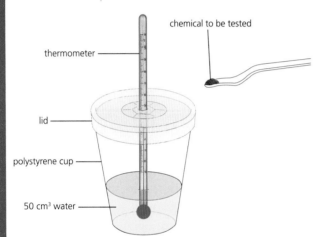 Karen and Lucy want to monitor the temperature changes as different chemicals dissolve in water. Each time they measure 50 cm^3 of water into a polystyrene cup, place a lid on the cup and poke a thermometer through the lid and into the water. One spatula of the chemical being tested is then added. Their results are shown below.

a) Which of the chemicals dissolved in endothermic processes?

b) Why are they using a polystyrene cup and not simply a beaker?

c) Suggest how Karen and Lucy could improve their experiment to make their results more accurate.

thermometer

chemical to be tested

lid

polystyrene cup

50 cm^3 water

Chemical dissolved	Temperature before adding (°C)	Temperature after adding (°C)
ammonium nitrate	20.2	7.6
potassium hydroxide	19.4	27.5
potassium chloride	20.7	18.4

Chemiluminescence

Chemiluminescence is the name given to the interesting phenomenon of light being produced by chemical reactions. Glow sticks demonstrate a fun application of chemiluminescence.

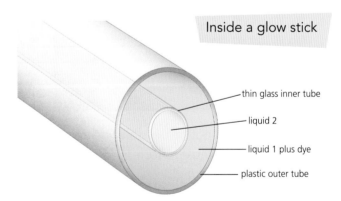

Inside a glow stick

thin glass inner tube

liquid 2

liquid 1 plus dye

plastic outer tube

Glow sticks demonstrate the idea of chemiluminescence

A glow stick is activated by bending the plastic outer tube. A thinner tube made of glass inside the plastic tube cracks and the two liquids mix. The chemical reaction that follows produces light for a few hours. The colour of the light seen depends on the dye used. ⇨

History of chemiluminescence

One of the earliest known examples of chemiluminescence is the oxidation of white phosphorus. The element phosphorus exists in two main forms, red phosphorus and white phosphorus. The first scientists to discover phosphorus (way back in the 1600s) noticed that it glowed with a slightly green colour when it was exposed to oxygen.

Modern uses

Luminol is a very useful chemical that displays chemiluminescence when it reacts with hydrogen peroxide.

Luminol in action

Luminol is used by **forensic investigators** at crime scenes to detect traces of blood that may have been left behind – even if someone has tried to clean the area. A chemical reaction between luminol and hydrogen peroxide which is catalysed by an iron compound present in blood produces a blue glow for 30 seconds or so. A solution containing luminol and hydrogen peroxide would be sprayed over the area under investigation while the room is dark, enabling the glow to be photographed.

Bioluminescence

Chemiluminescence is also present in nature where it is termed **bioluminescence**. Fireflies and their larvae (glow worms) emit light, perhaps to attract mates or as a defence mechanism to deter predators who would eat them. You might not be too keen to eat if your dinner glowed in the dark! The anglerfish uses bioluminescence for a very different reason. It uses a chemical reaction to create light very deep down in the ocean. As it is very dark, the light attracts smaller fish which the anglerfish lures in as prey.

Could you believe your eyes?

An anglerfish using bioluminescence to find food

Chemiluminescence

 Active Learning

Use the internet to research the work of Hennig Brand, the scientist who discovered phosphorus. Where did he get the phosphorus from? What was he trying to find? Find out some uses of phosphorus today.

QUESTIONS

1 What does chemiluminescence mean?

2 Light can be emitted through other processes. Find out about:
   a) incandescence
   b) fluorescence
   c) phosphorescence
   d) laser generation.

3 Luminol has been used at crime scenes for over 40 years.
   a) The glow occurs readily because iron behaves as a catalyst. What is a catalyst?
   b) Using luminol to detect blood is said to be a presumptive test. Find out what this means.
   c) Research other substances that may be found at a crime scene that would cause the same result in the luminol test as blood.

4 Find out about another creature that uses chemicals to produce light. Make a list of some of the reasons why the creature gives off light.

GLOSSARY

Calorimeter a piece of equipment used to measure heat in chemical reactions

Chemiluminescence the release of light energy as the result of a chemical reaction

Decomposes a compound breaking down into simpler chemical compounds or elements

Deflagrating spoon a special spoon used for heating a substance directly in a flame

Endothermic a process in which energy is taken in

Exothermic a process in which energy is released

Forensic investigator a scientist who tests materials to help with law enforcement

Oxidising agent a chemical that causes something else to be oxidised

Thermodynamics the study of the energy changes that result from chemical reactions

MATERIALS
Properties and uses of substances

6

No loss, no gain

Level 3 — What came before?

● **SCN 3-16b**

I have taken part in practical investigations into solubility using different solvents and can apply what I have learned to solve everyday practical problems.

Level 4 — What is this chapter about?

● **SCN 4-16b**

Through evaluation of experimental results, I can demonstrate my understanding of conservation of mass.

No loss, no gain

What is the matter?

All the matter on our planet is made from incredibly tiny particles called atoms. Over 2000 years ago a Roman called Lucretius wrote a book about the nature of the Universe as he saw it, and in the book, he described small separate particles which he called atoms. He took his ideas from even earlier thinkers, but these correct ideas were discredited when a famous philosopher, Aristotle, taught that all matter was derived from four 'elements' – Earth, Air, Fire and Water, with a fifth element, the Aether, which he decided filled the space between the stars. The 'four elements' theory was around long before Aristotle adopted it and unfortunately it is wrong, but because of Aristotle's reputation, his views were widely accepted and they were partly responsible for holding science back for nearly 2000 years!

Luckily, as the centuries passed the idea of matter being made of particles (as opposed to Aristotle's four elements) never quite went away, and by the eighteenth century it had moved back into the scientific mainstream. As with a lot of ideas and inventions, a number of people in different countries had similar ideas about atoms, but a scientist from the Lake District, John Dalton (see Chapter 1, page 7), is the one who is remembered as the man who published what is now called 'Dalton's Atomic Theory'.

Dalton is mentioned in Chapter 1 of this book. He is famous because he carried out a lot of quite accurate experiments, and in the first years of the nineteenth century he came up with the idea that 'the material world is made up of atoms of definite weight and size which have the power to rearrange in new ways'. His theory was accepted mainly because most scientists already agreed with him, but also because he stated that atoms of different elements had different masses and he was able to determine the atomic masses of a number of elements to a surprising degree of accuracy. Dalton had pointed chemistry in the right direction. His most important suggestions were:

- Atoms of each element are identical and are different from the atoms of all other elements.

- Atoms of different elements join up with each other in small, fixed, whole numbers. For example in water, H_2O, two hydrogen atoms join up with one oxygen atom: we say that the **ratio** of hydrogen to oxygen atoms is 2:1.

- Atoms cannot be created or destroyed, but they can be rearranged in a chemical reaction. We now know that atoms can, actually, be split into **sub-atomic particles** (electrons, protons and neutrons), but this does not happen during chemical reactions.

> *Active Learning*
>
> What is the difference between weight and mass? Find out and write a note which explains the difference.

Dalton's idea of atoms of different elements combining to make new substances known as compounds laid the foundation for modern chemistry because he gave each element known at the time its own symbol and he gave compounds formulae. This allowed people to write **chemical equations**.

Chemists say that chemical equations are the universal language of chemistry and that our vocabulary consists of symbols and formulae.

What is the matter?

We are just over 200 years away from Dalton's theory, and in those 200 years scientists have based thousands of new ideas on Dalton's original work. The application of these ideas has changed our lives dramatically. In the next section, we will look at how some of them have shaped modern society.

The Law of Conservation of Mass

The **Law of Conservation of Mass** says that 'no detectable gain or loss of mass occurs in chemical reactions'. In other words, the atoms that go into a reaction in the starting material (starting materials are called **reactants**) must all come out of the reaction in the material that is made (called the **products**). This law allows us to 'balance' chemical equations, and knowledge of atomic masses (these days called **relative atomic masses**) allows us to calculate exact quantities of material needed for chemical reactions: a fact that makes a lot of money for the big chemical companies.

Conservation of energy and mass

Energy can take different forms, including heat, light, sound, chemical and electrical energy. Energy can be converted from one form to another. You will already know about **exothermic** and **endothermic** reactions from Chapter 5. In some reactions, the reactants contain more chemical energy than the products, so the surplus energy is released to the surroundings. The energy released often makes the reaction mixture get warmer and we say that the reaction is exothermic. In other reactions, the reactants contain less energy than the products, so the reaction draws in energy from the surroundings. The reaction mixture often gets cooler and we say that the reaction is endothermic.

We now know that energy and mass can also be converted into each other according to Einstein's famous equation $E = mc^2$, but it needs a huge amount of energy to make even the tiniest change in mass, so even though some reactions release energy and others take it in, the Law of Conservation of Mass can still be applied to chemical reactions.

The following experiments and activities will investigate the Law of Conservation of Mass.

No loss, no gain

The Law of Conservation of Mass

Active Learning ▶

1 To find out how, and why, the mass of a candle changes when it burns.

(Your teacher may demonstrate this.)

Weigh a tea light and record its mass. Light the candle, leave it until the lesson is almost over then put an upturned beaker over the candle to extinguish it and measure its mass again. By subtraction, work out how the mass of the candle has changed while it has been burning.

Write your own explanation for the change in mass of the candle.

Design an experiment to show that burning a candle obeys the Law of Conservation of Mass.

QUESTIONS

1 What are modern candles made from?

2 Which elements are present in candle wax?

3 Why does the burning candle go out when a beaker is placed over it?

4 What is another name for burning?

5 What energy change occurs during an exothermic reaction?

2 To find out how, and why, the mass of a strip of magnesium changes when it burns.

(Your teacher may demonstrate this.)

Work out how the mass of the magnesium has changed in this experiment.

Write your own explanation for the change in mass of the magnesium.

QUESTIONS

1 Why, during the experiment on burning magnesium, did the crucible lid have to be tilted but not removed?

2 Why is it better to coil the magnesium before putting it in the crucible rather than fold it tightly into a small piece?

3 What are the two reactants in this chemical reaction?

Active Learning ▶

3 To find out how, and why, the mass of copper (II) carbonate changes when it is heated.

(Your teacher may demonstrate this.)

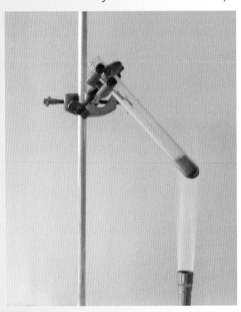

Calculate the mass of the green powder before heating and the mass of the remaining solid after heating and cooling.

Describe in your own words what you observed during this experiment and give your own explanation for the changes in colour and mass which took place.

4 To find out how, and why, the mass of copper (II) oxide changes when it is heated in a stream of methane gas.

(Your teacher may demonstrate this.)

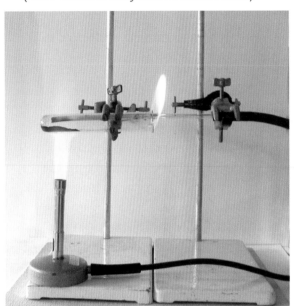

Calculate the mass of the copper (II) oxide before heating and the mass of the remaining solid after heating and cooling.

Describe in your own words what you observed during this experiment and give your own explanation for the changes in colour and mass which took place.

QUESTIONS

1 Why is it necessary to wait for a few seconds before igniting the gas?

2 What could the remaining solid be?

Chemical equations

A **chemical equation** is a short-hand way to describe a chemical reaction. Before we look at equations written using symbols and formulae, let us revisit the idea of word equations.

Word equations

A word equation uses the names of the chemicals instead of their symbols or formulae.

The names of all the substances we start off with (the reactants) are written on the left of the equation. The names of all the substances we end up with (the products) are written on the right of the equation. In between the reactants and the products we put an arrow which points towards the products. We do not use the 'equals' sign in chemical equations because the reactants do not equal the products. The reactants change into the products so an arrow, pointing from left to right (from reactants to products), is used.

Only the names of chemicals must be written in a word equation: words like powder, lumps, gas, vapour and heat are not the names of chemicals, so are not included.

Examples

1 When a small piece of shiny <u>sodium</u> metal is dropped into a jar of <u>chlorine</u> gas there is a flash of light and <u>sodium chloride</u> is formed.

It helps to underline the names of all the chemicals (elements and compounds) that appear in the description of the reaction. These are the only words you will need for the equation. Decide which chemicals you are starting with and which you are ending up with, then write the equation:

$$sodium + chlorine \rightarrow sodium\ chloride$$

2 When <u>carbon</u> is heated strongly, it catches fire and burns to make a gas called <u>carbon dioxide</u>.

There are only two chemicals named in this sentence, but you will know from previous work that when a substance burns, it reacts with a gas called oxygen. Oxygen is not actually mentioned in the sentence, but it must be included in the equation because it is taking part in the reaction.

The word equation for this reaction is:

$$carbon + oxygen \rightarrow carbon\ dioxide$$

The words 'gas' and 'heat' are not needed in the equation as they are not names of chemicals.

Active Learning ▶

Write word equations for each of these reactions:

1 If you roast (i.e. heat) iron sulphide strongly, it will react with oxygen from the air and form iron oxide and sulphur dioxide.

2 When natural gas, methane, is burned, a lot of heat energy is released as well as carbon dioxide gas and water vapour.

3 A yellow, insoluble solid called lead iodide is formed when solutions of potassium iodide and lead nitrate are mixed. A soluble compound, potassium nitrate, is also produced.

Balanced equations

If you wanted to bake a cake, you would need a recipe. This might tell you to start by mixing flour, sugar, butter, eggs and milk in a bowl. However, you need more information than that – what mass of flour, sugar and butter, how many eggs and what volume of milk should be measured out? If any of these quantities is wrong, the cake will not turn out well. Balanced chemical equations provide similar information about chemical reactions – they tell you how much of each reactant you need and how much of each product you will make.

$\Rightarrow$

You learned how to write chemical formulae in Chapter 1 of this book and you have already seen some chemical equations. Before we look at balancing equations in detail, let us just check that we can work out how many of each type of atom is present in a chemical formula.

Formula	Atoms present in the formula
HCl	one hydrogen atom and one chlorine atom
CO_2	one carbon atom and two oxygen atoms
HNO_3	one hydrogen, one nitrogen and three oxygen atoms
H_2SO_4	two hydrogen, one sulphur and four oxygen atoms
C_2H_5OH	two carbon, six hydrogen and one oxygen atom
CH_3COOH	two carbon, four hydrogen and two oxygen atoms

Each of the formulae above is for a **covalent** compound. Covalent compounds are made of **molecules**, each of which contains a set number of atoms. In the next set of examples, the formulae for some **ionic** compounds are given. Although it is not correct to talk about the number of atoms present in such formulae, this can be ignored for the purposes of the current work on equation balancing.

Formula	Atoms present in the formula
NH_4Cl	one nitrogen, four hydrogen and one chlorine atom
Na_3PO_4	three sodium, one phosphorus and four oxygen atoms
$Al(NO_3)_3$	one aluminium, three nitrogen and nine oxygen atoms
$Ca(HCO_3)_2$	one calcium, two hydrogen, two carbon and six oxygen atoms

Active Learning

In groups, take some spare paper and write down the correct formulae for five compounds; two that do not use brackets and three which do use brackets. Ask your teacher to check your group's formulae. Fold and exchange the paper with the group next to you. Unfold the papers. The first group to correctly work out the total number of atoms in all five compounds is the winner.

I'll lose my balance if I don't keep equal weight on both sides!

What does 'balancing' an equation mean?

It means there must be the same number of each type of atom in the products as there are in the reactants in order to obey the Law of Conservation of Mass.

The gas hobs and ovens in most houses burn natural gas. Natural gas is mostly methane, CH_4, so let us look at the chemical reaction commonly called the complete combustion of methane. The word equation is:

methane + oxygen → carbon dioxide + water

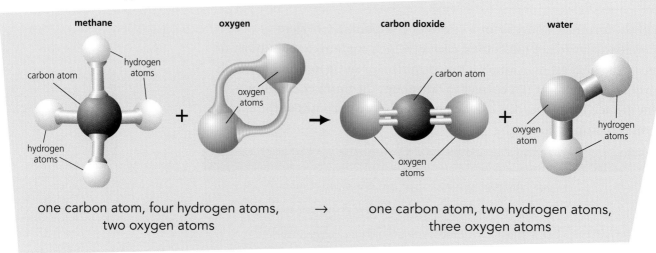

methane	**oxygen**	**carbon dioxide**	**water**

one carbon atom, four hydrogen atoms, two oxygen atoms → one carbon atom, two hydrogen atoms, three oxygen atoms

This equation does not obey the Law of Conservation of Mass, because during the reaction we seem to have destroyed two hydrogen atoms and created one oxygen atom. The equation is unbalanced.

We can correct this by putting a second oxygen molecule on the left-hand side of the equation and a second water molecule on the right.

$$CH_4 + O_2 \qquad\qquad \rightarrow \qquad\qquad CO_2 + H_2O$$
$$O_2 \qquad\qquad\qquad\qquad\qquad\qquad H_2O$$

one carbon atom, four hydrogen atoms, four oxygen atoms

one carbon atom, four hydrogen atoms, four oxygen atoms

The equation now has the correct number of each type of atom on the left and right of the arrow, and the balanced equation looks like this:

$$CH_4 + 2O_2 \rightarrow CO_2 + 2H_2O$$

The 'balancing number' 2 means two of everything up to the next + sign or up to the arrow.

Some examples

Remember: elements and compounds have fixed formulae and we cannot change them just to make balancing easier. If we want more of a particular atom on the left or right of the arrow, we have to add one or more complete formulae.

Reaction of sodium with water

1 The reaction of sodium with water produces sodium hydroxide and hydrogen. Write the balanced equation for this reaction.

We begin by writing the symbols and formulae for these substances, and then counting the 'atoms' to check whether or not the equation is balanced.

$Na + H_2O \rightarrow NaOH + H_2$ 2 H on left, 3 H on right, so

add H_2O 4 H on left, 3 H on right, so

add $NaOH$ 4 H on both sides now, but

1 Na on left, 2 Na on right, so

add Na

Written as a balanced equation, this becomes:

$2Na + 2H_2O \rightarrow 2NaOH + H_2$

2 Aluminium combining with oxygen.

$Al + O_2 \rightarrow Al_2O_3$ 1 Al on left, 2 Al on right, so

add Al   2 O on left, 3 O on right, so

add O_2 Now 4 O on left, 3 O on right, so

add Al_2O_3 Now 4 O on left, 6 O on right, so

add O_2 6 O on both sides now, but

2 Al on left, 4 Al on right, so

add Al + Al

Written as a balanced equation, this becomes:

$4Al + 3O_2 \rightarrow 2Al_2O_3$

Reaction of aluminium with oxygen

Numeracy   + − ÷ ×

Balance the following equations:

1 $N_2 + H_2 \rightarrow NH_3$

2 $NaOH + H_2SO_4 \rightarrow Na_2SO_4 + H_2O$

3 $Fe_2O_3 + CO \rightarrow Fe + CO_2$

4 $Na_2CO_3 + HNO_3 \rightarrow NaNO_3 + CO_2 + H_2O$

5 $CuO + CH_4 \rightarrow Cu + CO_2 + H_2O$

6 $C_3H_8 + O_2 \rightarrow CO_2 + H_2O$

No loss, no gain

Active Learning

Carry out, or watch your teacher demonstrate, each of the following experiments.

1 Collect a Bunsen burner, place it on a heat-proof mat and light it. Collect a piece of magnesium ribbon and some tongs. Using a blue flame, carefully burn the ribbon, keeping the ribbon over the heat-proof mat and avoiding looking directly at the flame.

When magnesium burns in oxygen, magnesium oxide is produced.

a) Write a word equation for the combustion (burning) of magnesium.

b) Write a balanced symbol equation for the combustion of magnesium.

2 Collect another piece of magnesium, a boiling tube, a test tube and some hydrochloric acid (an aqueous solution of hydrogen chloride). Pour approximately 5 cm^3 of hydrochloric acid into the test tube, add the magnesium and place the boiling tube upside-down over the test tube to collect the gas produced.

When magnesium reacts with hydrochloric acid, magnesium chloride and hydrogen are produced.

a) Write a word equation for the reaction between magnesium and hydrochloric acid.

b) Write a balanced symbol equation for the reaction between magnesium and hydrochloric acid.

3 The hydrogen gas you collected in experiment 2 can be identified, as it burns in oxygen with a squeaky pop, forming water.

Collect a splint, light it and hold it near the mouth of the boiling tube from experiment 2 to 'pop' the hydrogen gas.

a) Write a word equation for the reaction between hydrogen and oxygen.

b) Write a balanced symbol equation for the reaction between hydrogen and oxygen.

4 Collect some sodium carbonate powder and add a spatula load of it to approximately 2 cm^3 of hydrochloric acid. Observe the reaction.

When sodium carbonate reacts with hydrochloric acid, sodium chloride, carbon dioxide and water are produced.

a) How could you identify the gas produced?

b) Write a word equation for the reaction between sodium carbonate and hydrochloric acid.

c) Write a balanced symbol equation for the reaction between sodium carbonate and hydrochloric acid.

How much is used and how much is made?

For industrial chemists, the main point of balancing equations is to prevent waste. Chemicals are expensive so they use balanced equations to work out exactly how much reactant they need to start with in order to produce the required quantity of saleable product. If we are going to use chemical equations in this way, we first need to find a way of 'weighing out' atoms.

The masses of atoms

In Level 3 you found out that because atoms are so small, their masses are not measured in grams – we use a special unit called the **atomic mass unit** (amu) to describe their masses. A typical carbon atom has a mass of 12 amu. For experimental purposes we could never weigh this quantity of carbon. However, it is easy to weigh 12 **grams** of carbon. This is known as one **mole** of carbon.

The mole

One mole of an element is defined as the **relative atomic mass** (RAM) of that element measured in grams; the RAM is the average mass of one atom of the element. It is worth remembering that for diatomic elements, one mole is twice the RAM in grams. The RAMs of the elements are listed in data booklets. Some of them are not whole numbers because, although all atoms of the same element must have the same number of protons, they can have different numbers of neutrons so they can have different masses – there is no element for which all of the atoms weigh exactly the same. The average mass of an atom has therefore been calculated for each element. This figure is rounded up or down to the nearest whole number unless the calculation ends with a figure roughly midway between two numbers. This is why magnesium has a RAM of 24.5, chlorine 35.5 and copper 63.5, for example.

For compounds, one mole is the **relative formula mass** (RFM) weighed out in grams. The formula mass is the mass of all of the atoms in the formula added up.

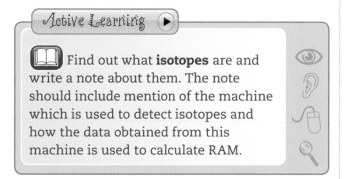

Active Learning ▶

📖 Find out what **isotopes** are and write a note about them. The note should include mention of the machine which is used to detect isotopes and how the data obtained from this machine is used to calculate RAM.

Formula mass and the mole

The formula mass of a compound is found by adding together the relative atomic mass of each atom in the formula. For example, the formula mass of water is calculated as follows:

a) write the formula for water H_2O

b) add up the mass of each atom $\quad 1 + 1 + 16 = 18$

c) the formula mass is $\quad 18$

d) so the mass of one mole of water is $\quad 18\,g$

Active Learning ▶

Using a data booklet, complete the following table. The first example has been done for you.

Substance	Formula	Formula mass	Mass of one mole
sulphuric acid	H_2SO_4	$1 + 1 + 32 + (4 \times 16) = 98$	98 g
lead			
argon			
oxygen			
carbon dioxide			
sulphur dioxide			
sodium hydroxide			
calcium carbonate			
magnesium nitrate			

Moles and calculations

Knowing how to measure quantities of reactants and products in grams allows us to make calculations based on balanced chemical equations. We can predict how much of a product we could make from a given mass of reactant, or calculate how much of a reactant we would need to make a certain mass of a product.

Calculations from equations

There are two main ways of doing these calculations:

1 using the ratio of reacting masses

2 converting masses to moles.

Using the ratio of reacting masses

1 Calculate the mass of carbon dioxide produced when 4 g of graphite (carbon) burns in air.

    a)   Write and balance the equation for the reaction.

$$C + O_2 \rightarrow CO_2$$

    b)   There will always be information about the quantity of one chemical in the question. Underline the formula of this chemical and write the quantity over the formula, then underline the formula of the chemical you have been asked about.

          4 g

$$\underline{C} \quad + \quad O_2 \quad \rightarrow \quad \underline{CO_2}$$

    c)   Write the ratio of moles beneath the formulae you have underlined and work out the ratio of reacting masses.

          4 g

$$\underline{C} \quad + \quad O_2 \quad \rightarrow \quad \underline{CO_2}$$

   1 mole   1 mole

   12 g $12 + (2 \times 16) = 44$ g

   12 g of carbon reacts with oxygen to give 44 g of carbon dioxide

   1 g of carbon reacts to give $\dfrac{44\,\text{g}}{12}$ of carbon dioxide

and 4 g of carbon reacts to give $\dfrac{(4 \times 44)\,\text{g}}{12}$ of carbon dioxide

                              $=$ $\underline{14.7\,\text{g}}$ of carbon dioxide

2 When hydrogen reacts with chlorine, hydrogen chloride is produced. Calculate the mass of hydrogen chloride which could be produced from 10 g of hydrogen.

a) H_2 + Cl_2 $\rightarrow$ 2HCl

b) 10 g

 $\underline{H_2}$ + Cl_2 $\rightarrow$ $\underline{2HCl}$

c) 1 mole   2 moles

 $(1 + 1)$ g $2 \times (1 + 35.5)$ g

 2 g   73 g

1 g of H_2 reacts to give $\dfrac{73 \text{ g}}{2}$ of hydrogen chloride

and 10 g of hydrogen reacts to give $\dfrac{(10 \times 73) \text{ g}}{2}$ of hydrogen chloride

$= \underline{365 \text{ g}}$ of hydrogen chloride

3 Calculate the mass of aluminium oxide produced when 1 kg of aluminium reacts with excess air (the word 'excess' means there is more than enough oxygen available).

a) 4Al + $3O_2$ $\rightarrow$ $2Al_2O_3$

b) 1000 g (1 kg)

 $\underline{4Al}$ + $3O_2$ $\rightarrow$ $\underline{2Al_2O_3}$

c) 4 moles   2 moles

 (4×27) g $2 \times [(27 \times 2) + (16 \times 3)]$ g

 108 g   204 g

1 g of aluminium reacts to give $\dfrac{204 \text{ g}}{108}$ of aluminium oxide

and 1000 g of aluminium reacts to give $\dfrac{(1000 \times 204) \text{ g}}{108}$ of aluminium oxide

$= \underline{1888.9 \text{ g}}$ or $\underline{1.9 \text{ kg}}$ of aluminium oxide

Converting masses to moles

4 Calculate the mass of aluminium oxide produced when 1 kg of aluminium reacts with excess air. Follow steps (a) and (b) as in **3** above. Then follow step (c) using moles as on the next page.

No loss, no gain

c) Calculate the number of moles of aluminium in 1 kg (1000 g) of the solid, then use the ratio of moles from the equation to find out how much product is made.

$$\underset{\substack{4\text{ moles}}}{4Al} \quad + \quad 3O_2 \quad \rightarrow \quad \underset{\substack{2\text{ moles}}}{2Al_2O_3}$$

1000 g above 4Al

Moles of aluminium $= \dfrac{mass}{mass\ of\ 1\ mole} = \dfrac{1000\,g}{27\,g} = 37.04$ moles

From the balanced equation:

4 moles Al $\rightarrow$ 2 moles Al_2O_3

so   2 moles Al   1 mole Al_2O_3

and   37.04 moles   18.52 moles Al_2O_3

Finally, mass of Al_2O_3 = moles × mass of 1 mole = 18.52 × 102 g

       = <u>1889.04 g</u> or <u>1.9 kg</u>

Numeracy   + − ÷ ×

Choose the method with which you feel more comfortable and try the following calculations. The answers to the calculations are given at the end of the section.

1 The equation for the complete combustion of methane is as follows:

$CH_4 + 2O_2 \rightarrow CO_2 + 2H_2O$

Calculate the mass of carbon dioxide produced by burning 4.0 g of methane.

2 What mass of calcium sulphate would be produced from 10.0 g of calcium chloride in the following reaction:

$CaCl_2(aq) + H_2SO_4(aq) \rightarrow CaSO_4(s) + 2HCl(aq)$

What type of reaction is this?

3 When calcium carbonate reacts with hydrochloric acid, calcium chloride, water and carbon dioxide are produced.

a) Write the balanced equation for this reaction.

b) What mass of calcium chloride would be produced if 20.0 g of calcium carbonate reacted with hydrochloric acid?

c) What type of reaction is this?

4 Iron can be made by reacting iron (III) oxide with carbon monoxide. Carbon dioxide is also produced.

a) Write a balanced equation for this reaction.

b) What mass of iron would be produced by reacting 100 tonnes of iron (III) oxide with excess carbon monoxide?

c) What type of reaction is this?

5 In the reaction between zinc and nitric acid, zinc (II) nitrate and hydrogen gas are formed.

a) Write a balanced equation for this reaction.

b) What mass of zinc nitrate would be produced from 32.5 g of zinc?

c) What type of reaction is this?

Answers

1 11 g
2 12.25 g
3 22.2 g
4 70 tonnes
5 94.5 g

GLOSSARY

Chemical equation a short-hand way of describing a chemical reaction; it shows how atoms or ions in the reactants rearrange themselves to form the products

Endothermic a process in which energy is taken in

Exothermic a process in which energy is released

Law of Conservation of Mass matter cannot be created or destroyed; in a chemical equation, the mass of the reactants must equal the mass of the products

Mole the quantity of a substance in grams calculated from its relative atomic mass or relative formula mass

Molecule a group of atoms held together by covalent bonds

Ratio the relationship of one quantity to another

Relative atomic mass the average mass of an atom of an element

Sub-atomic particles the smaller particles which make up atoms – protons, neutrons and electrons

PLANET EARTH
Processes of the planet

7

Going round in cycles

Level 3 — What came before?

 SCN 3-05b

I can explain some of the processes which contribute to climate change and discuss the possible impact of atmospheric change on the survival of living things.

Level 4 — What is this chapter about?

 SCN 4-05b

Through exploring the carbon cycle, I can describe the processes involved in maintaining the balance of gases in the air, considering causes and implications of changes in the balance.

 SCN 4-20b

Having selected scientific themes of topical interest, I can critically analyse the issues, and use relevant information to develop an informed argument.

Going round in cycles

You probably know that air is a mixture of gases. Five gases make up almost the entire mixture – nitrogen (78%), oxygen (21%), argon, carbon dioxide and water vapour (together less than 1%). Other gases are present in tiny quantities known as trace amounts. These gases have no colour or smell, so how do we know that they are present at all and how do we know the quantities present in the mixture known as air? Can these gases be made in the lab and tested? Yes! First, we will make oxygen.

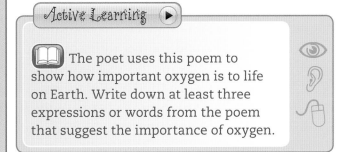

I am the very air you breathe, your first and last breath.

I welcomed you at birth. Shall bid farewell at death.

I am the Kiss of Life, its ebb and flow.

With your last gasp, you will call my name.

'O o o o o o o o'

Oxygen by Roger McGough

Active Learning ▶

The poet uses this poem to show how important oxygen is to life on Earth. Write down at least three expressions or words from the poem that suggest the importance of oxygen.

Oxygen is found in many chemical compounds. Oxides clearly contain oxygen and some oxides, for example, mercury (II) oxide and silver (I) oxide split up to produce metal and oxygen when heated. If your school has either of these oxides, this oxygen can be collected for testing. The names of some other compounds indicate the presence of oxygen as one of three or more elements. These compounds have names which end in 'ate' or 'ite', and a small number of them also produce oxygen when heated. One example commonly found in schools is potassium permanganate. When heated, this dark purple solid soon begins to crackle as it **decomposes**, producing oxygen.

Preparing, collecting and testing samples of oxygen

Ask your teacher how you might do this starting with potassium permanganate crystals. Learn how to collect gases by downward displacement of water. Collect at least two test tubes full of pure oxygen gas. Observe what happens when first a lit wooden splint is placed into a tube full of pure oxygen, and second when a glowing splint (one which you have set on fire and then blown out but kept glowing) is placed into another tube of the gas. Write a report of your experiment. Include a labelled diagram and a record of the results of your two tests.

What percentage of fresh air is oxygen?

This experiment is quick and easy to set up, but takes several days to produce a result. Take a chunk of steel wool, push it to the bottom of a measuring cylinder and add enough water to soak it. Pour away the excess water. Clamp the measuring cylinder upside down with the mouth of the cylinder dipping into some water contained in a large beaker or trough.

Air

During the days which follow, the steel wool will gradually rust. Part of this process involves the oxygen from the air in the cylinder being used up. As this happens, water from the beaker or trough will be drawn into the cylinder to replace the oxygen which has been 'lost'. Eventually, water will occupy about one-fifth (20%) of the volume of the cylinder.

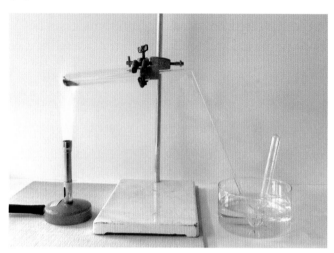

Active Learning ▶

Companies such as the British Oxygen Company (BOC) and Air Products make pure oxygen in extremely large quantities, but not by heating potassium permanganate!

Find out:

a) how these companies make oxygen

b) who their customers are and what they want pure oxygen for

c) why oxygen gas is transported as a liquid.

Preparing, collecting and testing samples of carbon dioxide

A similar method to that used to make oxygen can be used to make carbon dioxide. This time, however, you need to heat a carbonate compound. Although carbonates contain oxygen (indicated by the 'ate' at the end of the name), some of them produce carbon dioxide when heated rather than oxygen. Not all carbonates will work, but copper (II) carbonate does.

Using the apparatus shown above, heat some copper (II) carbonate and collect at least three test tubes of the carbon dioxide produced by downward displacement of water. Test one sample with a burning splint and another with a glowing splint in the same way as you did with oxygen. What happens? Now test a third tube of the gas with lime water. What happens? As before, write a report on your experiment. Include a diagram and the results of your tests.

Active Learning ▶

The same companies who manufacture oxygen also make and sell carbon dioxide. The method of production is the same as for oxygen. Find out who might buy carbon dioxide and what they might do with it.

Air

Percentage composition again

The quantities of most of the gases in air do not change – they are constant. However, for various reasons, the figures for oxygen, carbon dioxide and water vapour can change. For example:

- burning uses up oxygen while photosynthesis in plants produces it

- during respiration, plants and animals use up oxygen while generating energy; carbon dioxide and water are also produced in this reaction.

We may never be aware of any changes in the composition of the mixture, but some scientists believe that planet Earth is being affected by a slow but steady increase in the quantity of carbon dioxide in the air.

Is the planet's climate changing?

In January 2011, the World Meteorological Organisation declared that the first ten years of the new millennium had been the hottest decade since climate records began, and that 2010 had tied as the hottest year on record.

During 2010, there were many examples of extreme climatic conditions.

- In China, flooding and mud slides caused widespread disruption.

- In Russia the peat bogs dried out and caught fire as a result of the country's hottest summer on record. The toxic smog produced by the fires killed many people.

- In Canada they had the mildest winter ever recorded.

- In South America, record low temperatures were recorded.

- In Africa, millions of people were affected by drought.

- In Pakistan over 1500 people were killed and over 20 000 000 people were affected by the worst floods the country had experienced since records began.

- In Altnaharra in Sutherland, the temperature dropped to around –20 °C for several days, both in January and between November and December.

- In the Arizona desert in America, snow fell.

- In Australia, the state of Queensland suffered its worst floods in decades, with the water almost 10 metres deep in places. An area larger than France and Germany combined was affected.

Is the planet's climate changing?

In Level 3 you learned about some of the theories that scientists have which account for the apparent changes in the world's climate. Although not everyone agrees, one of the most commonly advanced explanations is the gradual increase in the temperature of planet Earth caused by a vast increase in the quantity of carbon dioxide gas in our atmosphere. This results from our use of fossil fuels (which release the gas when they are burned) alongside the chopping down of rainforests (which absorb it) and damage to the ozone layer (resulting in the destruction of plankton in the oceans which also absorb it). In order to form an opinion regarding this issue, we will now investigate what is known as the carbon cycle.

> *I am an atom of carbon, and carbon is the key;*
> *I am the element of life, and you owe yours to me.*
> *I am the glue of the universe, the fixative used by the great model maker.*
> *I play a waiting game – lie low, that's my secret.*
> *Take a breath, every millennium.*
> *But though set in my ways, don't be misled – I'm not inert.*
> *I will go down in cosmic history as an adventurer.*
> *For when I do make a move, things happen – and fast.*
> *I am an atom of carbon, and carbon is the key;*
> *I am the element of life, and you owe yours to me.*
> *When the tune is called, I carry the message to the piper;*
> *Take the lead in the decorous dance of life and death.*
> *Patient, single minded and stable, I keep my talents hidden.*
> *Bide my time, until by time am bidden.*
>
> *Carbon* by Roger McGough

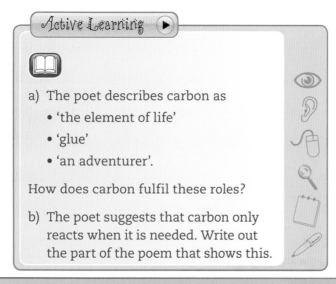

Active Learning

a) The poet describes carbon as
   - 'the element of life'
   - 'glue'
   - 'an adventurer'.

   How does carbon fulfil these roles?

b) The poet suggests that carbon only reacts when it is needed. Write out the part of the poem that shows this.

The life and times of a carbon atom

One day I was set on fire as part of a lump of coal. As a result I floated off into the atmosphere as a molecule of carbon dioxide and drifted off in the wind. Some time later while visiting Scotland I was absorbed by a barley plant through one of its green leaves and, before I knew it, I had become part of a glucose molecule. Life was sweet, but soon the crop was harvested. The entire crop was mashed up with some yeast in warm water by machinery. Having been part of a lump of solid and then part of a gaseous molecule, I was now part of a liquid molecule known as ethanol. Left to mature in an oak barrel for several years, I was eventually bottled as Scotland's national drink – whisky! One day, my bottle was opened and someone poured some whisky – freedom! I landed somewhere extremely cold – it felt like ice. Next thing, I felt like I was drowning as water was added to my new home – a glass. I found my way to the surface and was able to evaporate, just before I was swallowed by someone! Then my journey continued.

The number of carbon atoms on Earth, while impossible to calculate, is constant. Carbon forms the basis of all life since it is part of **DNA**.

The average human body contains 10 kilograms or more of carbon in one form or another. Carbon atoms in our bodies today will have formed parts of many other molecules in previous ages, going back to the beginning of time.

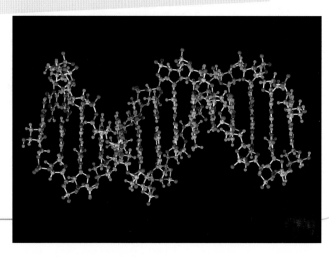

You have probably heard people say that milk is good for you because it contains calcium, which is good for your bones and teeth. It is true that milk, bones and teeth do contain calcium, but not as an element – they all contain calcium compounds. Although carbon is found on planet Earth as an element, it is also found in many compounds and in many places:

- as carbon dioxide in the atmosphere

- as organic molecules in living and dead organisms

- as organic matter in soils

- as fossil fuels

- as sedimentary rock deposits such as limestone and chalk

- as dissolved carbon dioxide in the oceans

- as calcium carbonate shells in marine organisms.

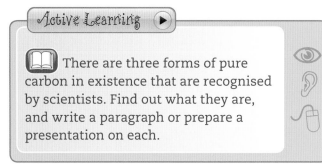

Active Learning ▶

There are three forms of pure carbon in existence that are recognised by scientists. Find out what they are, and write a paragraph or prepare a presentation on each.

The carbon cycle

Carbon cycles exist both in the atmosphere and in the oceans. We will look first at the carbon cycle on land and in the atmosphere.

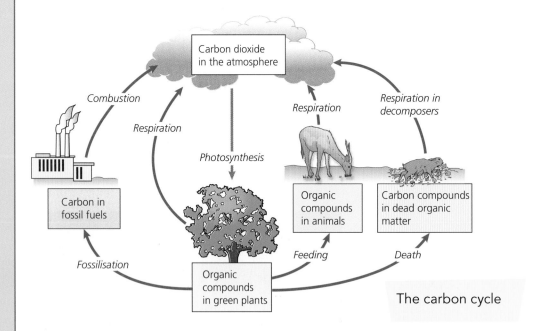

The carbon cycle

The carbon cycle

As mentioned in the little story earlier, the burning of fossil fuels produces carbon dioxide which, through photosynthesis, results in the production of carbohydrates in plants. Thus a carbon atom which was part of a carbon dioxide molecule becomes part of a glucose molecule and ultimately a starch molecule. What happens next could be one of several things:

- The plants could be used as fuel. For example, in Mauritius **carbon neutral** electricity is generated by burning bagasse, which is a material extracted from sugar cane, to power the generators. This results in carbon dioxide being returned to the atmosphere, but the next cane crop will use it during photosynthesis.

- The plants could be eaten by animals, which in turn may be eaten by other animals in a food chain. During respiration these animals obtain energy from the plants while also producing carbon dioxide as a waste product. This is released back into the atmosphere in the exhaled air of the animals. When animals and plants die, carbon dioxide is returned to the atmosphere through decomposition. New plants can use this carbon dioxide to grow.

- Alcoholic drinks can be made from plants. The 'alcohol' in these drinks is a carbon compound known as ethanol.

All of this means that carbon atoms seem to be recycled continually. Theoretically the quantity of carbon dioxide in the atmosphere should remain constant. However, if it does not, dramatic changes could result, so it is important to understand how the carbon cycle works in order to appreciate the danger of it not working.

Another carbon cycle is to be found in the oceans, which make up about 70% of the surface of planet Earth.

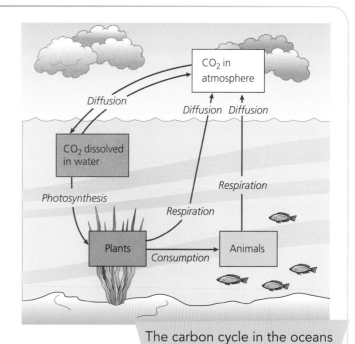

The carbon cycle in the oceans

If climate change is caused by the build-up of man-made carbon dioxide and other greenhouse gases in the atmosphere, it is important to understand what causes the build-up. In the case of carbon dioxide, the rate of build-up depends on how much CO_2 we emit and how much of it is absorbed by plants and soil or is transported down into the ocean depths by plankton (microscopic plants and animals). Scientists believe that the oceans currently absorb up to half of the CO_2 produced by the burning of fossil fuels. If they did not do this, atmospheric CO_2 levels would be much higher than the current level. Phytoplankton (microscopic plants) absorb CO_2 during photosynthesis. Carbon dioxide enters the waters of the ocean by **diffusion**. Once dissolved in seawater, the carbon dioxide can remain dissolved in the water as molecules:

$$CO_2(g) + H_2O(l) \rightarrow CO_2(aq)$$

Phytoplankton can use this CO_2 during photosynthesis. Some of the carbon compounds produced end up deep down in the ocean in the remains of dead plants and animals which have eaten the phytoplankton. The remains then become buried in the ocean sediment. Over time, these materials decay, resulting in CO_2 being released back into the water, where most of it dissolves. Currents in the ocean can bring the dissolved gas to the surface where it may either be absorbed once again by phytoplankton or returned to the atmosphere by diffusion from the ocean surface. However, carbon dioxide can also **react** with water to form carbonic acid:

$$CO_2(g) + H_2O(l) \rightarrow H_2CO_3(aq)$$

The carbonic acid splits up to produce hydrogencarbonate ions (also known as bicarbonate ions):

$$H_2CO_3(aq) \rightarrow H^+(aq) + HCO_3^-(aq)$$

which can also split forming carbonate ions:

$$HCO_3^-(aq) \rightarrow H^+(aq) + CO_3^-(aq)$$

Some forms of sea life combine these ions with calcium (Ca^{2+}) ions to produce calcium carbonate ($CaCO_3$). This substance is used to produce shells and other body parts by organisms such as coral, clams and oysters.

Some of the undersea creatures which use carbonates to make body parts

When these organisms die, their shells and body parts sink to the ocean floor. After long periods of time, these deposits become sedimentary rocks.

Active Learning

Is it possible to prove that seashells contain calcium carbonate?

1 Carbonate compounds react with acids to produce carbon dioxide gas. Design an experiment in which acid is added to shells, with the gas produced being tested for carbon dioxide.

2 The presence of some metals in compounds can be shown by doing a flame test. Find out which metals give colours to flames. Make a list of some of them and then ask your teacher if you can flame test some crushed shells to show that they contain calcium.

3 What about egg shells? Repeat these tests using egg shells to find out whether they contain calcium carbonate.

4 Redraw the diagram of the carbon cycle in the oceans (page 83) and add to it using the information given in the paragraph below the diagram.

Could the oceans do more to help?

There are large areas of ocean in which photographs taken from satellites show quite high phytoplankton growth.

This satellite picture from the European Space Agency shows the swirls of phytoplankton blooms off the coast of Ireland.

It is thought that the rapid growth of phytoplankton was caused by increased levels of certain chemicals in the water, brought there in dust from the 2010 volcanic eruption in Iceland.

However, other areas of the ocean show quite low phytoplankton growth. These have come to be known as High-Nutrient Low-Chlorophyll (HNLC) regions because they have high levels of nutrients such as phosphorus and nitrogen but have low chlorophyll concentrations (in other words, few phytoplankton). It was originally thought that hungry **zooplankton** (microscopic animals which feed on phytoplankton) were responsible for the low levels of phytoplankton, but research has shown that it is because those areas are lacking in a **micronutrient** required for plankton growth – iron. Theoretically, if we could add iron to these areas, more phytoplankton would grow and absorb even more CO_2 from the atmosphere by photosynthesis. A famous American oceanographer, John Martin, once said 'Give me half a tanker of iron and I'll give you an ice age!' His theory was that adding the missing micronutrient could promote the growth of so much phytoplankton that the quantity of CO_2 which would be absorbed by photosynthesis would be vast enough to put global warming into reverse!

Active Learning ▶

📖 Find out where these HNLC regions are. Write a report describing how scientists tested the effect of adding iron to water on phytoplankton growth.

On 3 December 2010 His Royal Highness Prince Charles opened a new climate change exhibition at the Science Museum in London.

Prince Charles at the climate change exhibition

Dr Robert Mulvaney OBE, glaciologist at the British Antarctic Survey who contributed to the exhibition, said, 'Seeing or holding a piece of ice that fell as snowfall, tens, hundreds, or even hundreds of thousands of years ago, and being able to see for yourself the bubbles of ancient air trapped within it, is like travelling back in time and is a significant moment for anyone – including the climate scientists.'

Could the oceans do more to help?

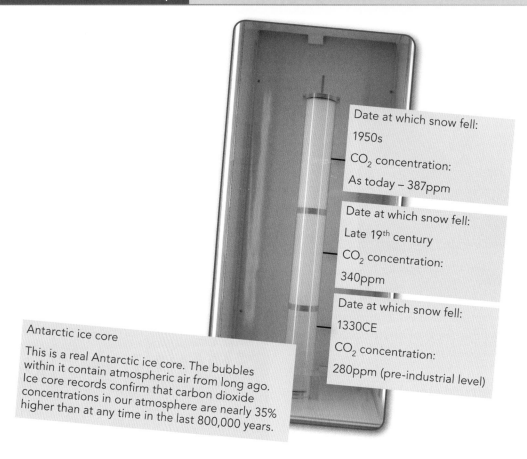

Date at which snow fell:
1950s

CO_2 concentration:
As today – 387ppm

Date at which snow fell:
Late 19th century

CO_2 concentration:
340ppm

Date at which snow fell:
1330CE

CO_2 concentration:
280ppm (pre-industrial level)

Antarctic ice core

This is a real Antarctic ice core. The bubbles within it contain atmospheric air from long ago. Ice core records confirm that carbon dioxide concentrations in our atmosphere are nearly 35% higher than at any time in the last 800,000 years.

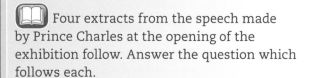 Active Learning

Four extracts from the speech made by Prince Charles at the opening of the exhibition follow. Answer the question which follows each.

1 'Alas, however, as you know only too well, climate science has taken a battering of late. It is why I specifically paid a visit to the School of Environmental Sciences at the University of East Anglia earlier this year. It is home to the Climatic Research Unit and I have been its Patron for nearly twenty years. I wanted to discuss with them the appalling treatment they had endured during the so-called "Climategate" row because, as they reminded me, the University of East Anglia is not a campaigning NGO, nor an industry lobby group. It is an academic institution working to understand precisely and dispassionately what is happening to our world; to separate the facts from the fiction and build the sum of human knowledge on the one issue that could very well balloon into the cause of our downfall.'

Prince Charles refers to 'Climategate' at the University of East Anglia. Find out about this incident and write a report on it.

2 'On my visit, I was given a briefing on the latest hard facts of science and it is all thoroughly depressing. We now have a pretty clear picture of what is happening

Active Learning ▶

as a result of human activity and that allows us to build reliable models that chart the risks we take with our children and grandchildren's future if we carry on with business as usual. Emissions of greenhouse gases will continue to rise – they are doing so now – and so we all must decide what we do about it.'

Find out about the agreement on greenhouse gas emissions reached in Mexico in December 2010.

3 'The great irony, of course, of all this anti-science stuff is that here I am endlessly supporting the science of climate change, when it is being vigorously and ruthlessly opposed by all those whom you would have thought were vigorously "pro-science" in every shape and form!'

Who do you think he might be referring to as the people who produce 'anti-science stuff' who should be 'vigorously "pro-science"'?

4 'The public needs to understand science much better than they do. This was brought into sharp focus for me earlier this summer when I read a survey which showed that nearly 60 per cent of the population no longer trusts scientists to tell the truth about controversial scientific and technological issues because, and I quote, "scientists depend more and more on money from industry". If this is so, then the scientific community has a big problem that could block important progress on something as crucial as climate change.'

Prince Charles talks about the belief that money provided by industry to fund scientific research could possibly influence the outcome of that research. The climate change exhibition was paid for by an oil company, at a cost of £4.5 million. Do you think there is a conflict of interest here? Explain your answer.

GLOSSARY

Carbon neutral not adding carbon dioxide to the atmosphere

Decompose a reaction in which a chemical breaks down into smaller ones without reacting with another chemical

Diffusion the movement of molecules between, for example, the atmosphere and the ocean

DNA deoxyribonucleic acid

Micronutrient an element required in tiny quantities for plants to grow

PLANET EARTH

Biodiversity and interdependence
Chemical changes
Energy sources and sustainability

8

The solution for pollution?

Level 3   What came before?

 SCN 3-18a

Having taken part in practical activities to compare the properties of acids and bases, I have demonstrated ways of measuring and adjusting pH and can describe the significance of pH in everyday life.

Level 4   What is this chapter about?

 SCN 4-03a

Through investigating the nitrogen cycle and evaluating results from practical experiments, I can suggest a design for a fertiliser, taking account of its environmental impact.

 SCN 4-04a

By contributing to an investigation on different ways of meeting society's energy needs, I can express an informed view on the risks and benefits of different energy sources, including those produced from plants.

 SCN 4-18a

I can monitor the environment by collecting and analysing samples. I can interpret the results to inform others about levels of pollution and express a considered opinion on how science can help to protect our environment.

The solution for pollution?

Air today, gone tomorrow

The composition of the air that we breathe is very important to life on our planet. Many of the chemical processes that living things carry out rely on different elements being available in the correct quantities. Air is mostly a mixture of nitrogen and oxygen with traces of other gases as shown below.

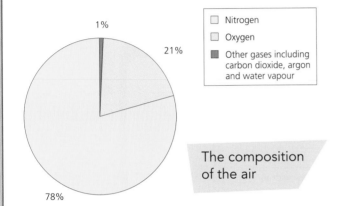

Legend:
☐ Nitrogen
☐ Oxygen
■ Other gases including carbon dioxide, argon and water vapour

1%, 21%, 78%

The composition of the air

While pollution can occur naturally, humans have been responsible for polluting the air for many years. Natural pollution can arise from occurrences like volcanic eruptions, where particles of chlorine and sulphur are ejected into the air, or more commonly from the methane produced by grazing animals (like cattle or sheep) when digesting their food.

Much of the pollution caused by humans is related to **combustion** reactions. What happens in a combustion reaction?

Power plants, factories, cars, ships and aircraft all operate by burning **fossil fuels**. As these contain carbon, carbon dioxide will be produced. Incomplete combustion may result in the production of carbon monoxide. Sulphur is commonly present as an impurity in fossil fuels and thus sulphur dioxide can also be produced when fuels derived from fossil fuels burn.

In addition to the harmful gases, **particulate matter** (small, light particles of a solid or liquid) is also released into the environment. The smaller and lighter these particles are, the longer they will stay in the air and the further they can travel. The most common particulate matter in urban areas is soot, produced from the incomplete combustion of hydrocarbon fuels. Exhaust gases from diesel-fuelled vehicles contain a lot of carbon soot. This can often be seen as the black discolouration around shiny exhaust pipes.

The solution for pollution?

Particulate matter is responsible for health problems as these particles can enter our bodies easily. Breathing poor quality air has been linked to asthma, heart disease and cancer. A study in 2000 by the European Commission linked more than 32 000 premature deaths in the UK every year to particulate matter. Particles breathed in can enter our respiratory system and bloodstream. It is not unusual to see cyclists in inner cities wearing masks to prevent inhalation of these harmful materials.

QUESTIONS

1 Data was collected from Scotland's main cities in 2008 about their particulate matter (PM) outputs. The results are shown in the graph below.

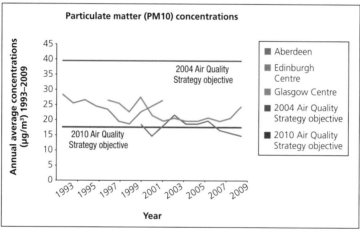

Source: Scotland Air Quality Data and Statistics Database,
http://www.scotland.gov.uk/Topics/Statistics/Browse/Environment/TrendPM10

a) Which city is least likely to have met the 2010 emissions target?

b) In which year were the emission levels the same in the centres of Glasgow and Edinburgh?

c) Why do you think Aberdeen's levels are consistently lower than those of the other two cities?

d) What was the highest average concentration recorded?

2 Why do you think that there is more pollution due to cow methane than there was 20 years ago? What developments have caused this?

3 Soot is described as being colloid. Find out what this term means.

4 Research the studies into air quality in Scotland. Find monitoring data for your area about particulate matter levels.

Water pollution

Many of the waste gases we release into the air result in further pollution problems when they dissolve in rain clouds. Acidic gases produced from combustion of fossil fuels are soluble in water. Once dissolved, acid rain is produced. The pH of acid rain is lower than that of natural rainwater.

Active Learning ▶

Try to monitor the pH of rainfall in your area. Each day you could check the rainfall and record important information about it. A simple acid rain collector can be built from a 2-litre juice bottle that has been cut in half. Making a liner for this bottle from a plastic bag will allow it to be changed daily. Begin your study and every day change the bag, collecting and measuring the pH and volume of any rainwater collected (there should be plenty in Scotland!). An important consideration is where to place your acid rain collector. Water should be able to be collected from rainfall but it will have to be somewhere free from contamination (such as water dripping from tree branches or roofs of houses) and also safe enough that it will not be knocked over. Share the results of your study. You may wish to give a presentation so think about how to present your results. Produce charts or graphs representing your data.

Why is natural rainwater slightly acidic?

When carbon dioxide dissolves in water it forms carbonic acid, a weak acid. This can be represented by the following equation:

carbon dioxide + water $\rightleftharpoons$ carbonic acid

$$CO_2(g) + H_2O(l) \rightleftharpoons H_2CO_3(aq)$$

The arrows used above are different from the arrow normally used in equations. They show that the reaction is reversible and works both ways. While carbonic acid is being formed from the reactants, some carbonic acid already present is also breaking down to reform carbon dioxide and water. Carbonic acid is a weak acid. Since there is some carbon dioxide in our atmosphere, all rainwater is slightly acidic though not acidic enough to cause serious damage to our environment. It has a pH of around 5–6.

What causes 'acid rain' then? Most scientists consider rainwater with a pH of less than 5 to be acid rain. Other gases dissolving in rain clouds must be responsible for this. The main pollutants are sulphur dioxide and nitrogen dioxide.

Sulphur dioxide

When sulphur dioxide is released into the atmosphere, it reacts with oxygen to form another gas called sulphur trioxide.

sulphur dioxide + oxygen → sulphur trioxide

$$SO_2(g) + O_2(g) \rightarrow SO_3(g)$$

(Could you balance this equation?)

Sulphur trioxide then reacts with water to form sulphuric acid.

sulphur trioxide + water → sulphuric acid

$$SO_3(g) + H_2O(l) \rightarrow H_2SO_4(aq)$$

Nitrogen dioxide

Nitrogen is a very unreactive gas. It requires a lot of energy to be input for it to react. There are times, however, when nitrogen reacts with oxygen in the air to form nitrogen monoxide and nitrogen dioxide. For example, in an electrical storm the energy needed to make this happen comes from bolts of lightning.

Nitrogen dioxide is a very soluble acidic gas that reacts with water as shown below to form nitric acid.

nitrogen dioxide + water → nitric acid + nitrogen monoxide

$$3NO_2(g) + H_2O(l) \rightarrow 2HNO_3(aq) + NO(g)$$

Both sulphuric acid and nitric acid are strong acids and will therefore significantly lower the pH of rainwater.

QUESTIONS

1 Stephen and Amy tested the pH of rainwater collected near their school. They found that the rainwater turned universal indicator yellow.

  a) What pH was the rainwater?

  b) What has caused the pH of the rainwater to be lower than 7?

  c) Based on their results, do you think acid rain is a problem in their area? Explain your answer.

2 How can we prevent the release of harmful acidic gases into our environment?

3 What effects do you think acid rain could have on your local area? Would there be any visible damage?

Fertilisers: helping nature feed the world

Fertilisers are substances added to soil to help crops grow. You should know a bit about them from Level 3. Fertilisers can be either natural (compost or manure) or synthetic. Synthetic fertilisers are also referred to as NPK fertilisers because they provide nitrogen, phosphorus and potassium to growing plants. Synthetic fertilisers can be an expensive way of ensuring plant growth, but as the population of our planet increases, so does the demand for food.

Active Learning

Use the internet to research how the global population has grown in the last 150 years. What effect do you think this will have on natural resources? What are the main issues faced by future generations because of the massive increases in population in the last 15–20 years?

Fertilisers: helping nature feed the world

Natural fertilisers play an important role in the nitrogen cycle by returning nitrates to the soil.

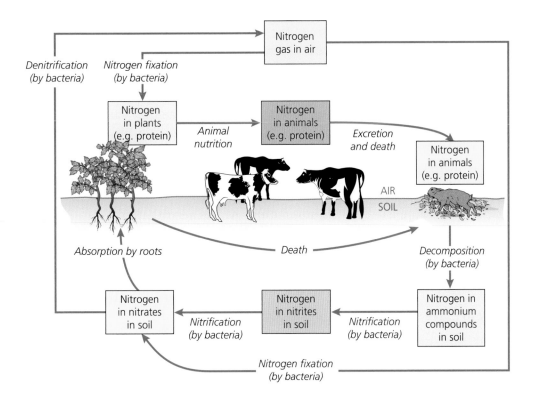

Nitrates are removed from the soil by plants during growth. Animals in turn eat the crops and the eventual death and decay (of the animal or the uneaten crop) returns the nitrates to the soil so that the cycle can continue. The cycle is interrupted when crops are harvested by humans and the nitrates do not make their way naturally back into the soil. This creates the need for artificial fertilisers.

Fertilisers can be made by **neutralisation** reactions. Remember that in a neutralisation reaction, an acid and a **base** (often an alkali) react together to produce a salt and water. Choosing a different acid or alkali will change the salt produced. The salt takes the first part of its name from the base and the end of its name from the acid used.

Name of acid	Salt name ends with...
hydrochloric acid	...chloride
sulphuric acid	...sulphate
nitric acid	...nitrate
phosphoric acid	...phosphate

The solution for pollution?

Active Learning

Designing a fertiliser

For a fertiliser to be effective, it must contain one or more of the three nutrients essential for plant growth. These nutrients (the elements nitrogen, phosphorus and potassium) are needed for the plant to make proteins, chlorophyll and sugars.

Fertilisers can be produced by neutralisation reactions. Which acid would you choose and why? Nitric acid (HNO_3) produces nitrate salts when neutralised. Choosing a base that will supply another of the essential plant nutrients will make the fertiliser more effective. Be careful! If the product of your neutralisation reaction is insoluble then it cannot be used as a fertiliser. How will you be able to tell that the acid has been neutralised? How could your fertiliser be extracted from any water that was also produced?

Example: ammonium sulphate $(NH_4)_2SO_4$ is a salt that is commonly used as a synthetic fertiliser. It can be produced when sulphuric acid is neutralised by ammonia solution:

$$\text{sulphuric acid} + \text{ammonia} \rightarrow \text{ammonium sulphate}$$

$$H_2SO_4(aq) + 2NH_3(aq) \rightarrow (NH_4)_2SO_4(aq)$$

Ask your teacher if you can try to make some ammonium sulphate.

QUESTIONS

1 A local garden centre has a number of different chemicals on display in their fertilisers section.

Fertiliser name	Formula	No. of bags sold
Jables Grows	NH_4NO_3	88
Tenth Prestige	$Ca_3(PO_4)_2$	19
Nelly's Nutrients	K_3PO_4	67

a) Suggest a reason why Tenth Prestige is the least popular fertiliser.

b) Which fertiliser would you recommend to customers of the garden centre? Explain your answer.

c) Draw a bar graph representing the sales of these fertilisers.

2 Julie wants to make a fertiliser in the lab. She has solutions of the following chemicals available: nitric acid (HNO_3), hydrochloric acid (HCl), phosphoric acid (H_3PO_4), sodium hydroxide (NaOH) and potassium hydroxide (KOH).

a) Which acid and alkali, if chosen together, would produce a compound that would **not** provide the necessary plant nutrients?

b) Describe a method she could follow to complete the neutralisation reaction needed to make a fertiliser.

c) Choose an acid and alkali from her list and write the word and symbol equations for the reaction between them.

d) How could she obtain a dry sample of the fertiliser she had made?

The sea's disease: fertilisers and water pollution

Excessive use of fertilisers can also be responsible for water pollution. For a compound to be suitable as a fertiliser it must be soluble so that it can be easily delivered to the roots of the plants. If too much fertiliser is left on the top layer of soil, rainwater can wash the fertiliser away and the soluble compounds used to promote healthy plant growth can find their way back into water supplies, potentially damaging pond life. These 'run-off' fertilisers deliver nutrients into water, where the higher concentration of phosphates in particular can cause algae to grow. While algae are not classed as plants, they are simple organisms and nearly all make food by photosynthesis.

Algal blooms occur when algae grow rapidly, encouraged by the addition of the nutrients from fertilisers. The main pollution problem arises when algae, which have a very short life-span, die and the dead organic matter begins to decay. The decaying process removes oxygen from the water affecting the survival of both fish and plants.

For life to flourish in water, the water needs to contain a high concentration of dissolved oxygen. If the concentration of oxygen in the water is too low, the water becomes **hypoxic** and fish cannot usually survive.

A 'fish kill' like this shows the widespread disruption to water-dwelling life

Algae grow rapidly when phosphates are present

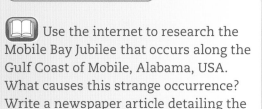

Active Learning ▶

Use the internet to research the Mobile Bay Jubilee that occurs along the Gulf Coast of Mobile, Alabama, USA. What causes this strange occurrence? Write a newspaper article detailing the event.

The solution for pollution?

Protecting our environment

As we have seen in this chapter, we are responsible for harming our environment in many different ways. It is our responsibility as scientists not only to monitor pollution levels and ensure regulation of the waste products we release into the environment but also to find safer alternatives to the processes that are causing damage to our planet.

Not all pollution arises through our everyday use of chemicals. Accidents like oil tankers crashing and deep ocean pipelines bursting are also responsible for releasing unwanted chemicals into our water supplies. In October 2010 a dam burst at a Hungarian chemical plant which specialises in refining bauxite (an aluminium ore) into aluminium oxide. The residue of this process was stored by the dam but was released as a red toxic sludge into the local area. The accident resulted in the deaths of at least nine people with around 120 people injured and many more evacuated from the area. Toxic heavy metals such as chromium, arsenic and mercury were released in small volumes by the spill. The sludge also contained sodium oxide (Na_2O) which gave the sludge a high pH and was responsible for causing chemical burns to people who had come into direct contact with it. The sludge reached the Danube River (Europe's second longest river) and it was initially feared that it would spread to a much greater area.

To counteract the high pH of the sludge, which at one point was as high as 12, emergency workers poured large quantities of acid and clay into streams in an effort to lower the pH. They managed to re-establish a safer pH of 8, but the clean-up operation had to continue into the following year at an estimated cost of £64 million.

QUESTIONS

1 Imagine you are responsible for health and safety at a chemical plant that produces large volumes of acid. What safety measures would you put in place for your workers and what precautions would you take against possible spillages and leaks?

2 Further dangers were presented in the Hungarian incident by the sludge drying out. The toxic elements present in the sludge would exist as dust on top of the dried layer and could be breathed in, causing respiratory problems. Design a poster highlighting the dangers of breathing in particulate matter.

3 When oil is spilled into water, both wildlife and human lives are put in danger. Research an oil spill and write an article for a national newspaper highlighting the dangers caused, how much oil was spilled and what the clean-up involved.

The toxic red sludge released by the bursting of the dam

Pollution-free fuels?

Burning hydrocarbon fuels will always result in carbon dioxide being produced. Several alternatives to conventional petrol or 'dinosaur diesel' are already available and widely used. While each may have benefits there are other important considerations.

Buses that run on old vegetable oil in Ayrshire

Between 2009 and 2010 the bus company Stagecoach piloted what is known as a Bio Bus.

The Bio Bus

Running between the towns of Darvel and Stewarton in East Ayrshire, these buses do not use traditional diesel fuel, but run on **biodiesel** made from used cooking oil and other food industry by-products collected from homes and restaurants. Containers to collect the cooking oil were given free to people living in houses on the bus route. The oil was taken to a recycling plant and people were given discounted travel on the Bio Bus in return. Stagecoach calculated that this cut carbon dioxide emissions from the buses by 80% and removed over 1000 tonnes of carbon dioxide from the atmosphere.

Numeracy + − ÷ ×

1 One tonne is known as a 'metric ton'. Find out exactly what the difference is between 1 tonne and 1 ton.

2 How much carbon dioxide was emitted before the introduction of Bio Buses if the 1000 tonnes reduction represented exactly 80%?

Active Learning ▶

1 Clearly there is something good about making use of all this old oil and fat rather than disposing of it, but what are the other benefits of biodiesel? Try to find out and make a list.

2 Suppose that companies started to grow crops which produce oil for converting to biodiesel on land which is currently used to grow food crops. Is this ethical? This sounds like a reason for not pursuing the production of biodiesel. What do you think? Make a list of other reasons against the use of biodiesel.

3 Where does the name 'diesel' come from? Research and write a newspaper article on the work of Rudolf Diesel.

Pollution-free fuels?

How is cooking oil turned into biodiesel?

Clearly you cannot just pour old cooking oil into the fuel tanks of buses. Apart from anything else, they would smell like mobile chip shops! So how is the biodiesel made?

Argent Energy UK opened the first large-scale biodiesel plant in 2005 near Motherwell. At the plant, biodiesel is made from tallow (animal fat) and used cooking oil using a type of alcohol called methanol and a catalyst. After the chemical reaction the biodiesel is distilled to ensure it reaches the British quality standard. Normally it is mixed with petrodiesel (diesel obtained from crude oil) and so what you can buy on the forecourts of petrol stations today is petrodiesel with up to 7% biodiesel, known as B7. However, the Stagecoach buses in East Ayrshire run on pure biodiesel (B100) produced by Argent. The plant can produce about 50 million litres of biodiesel per year.

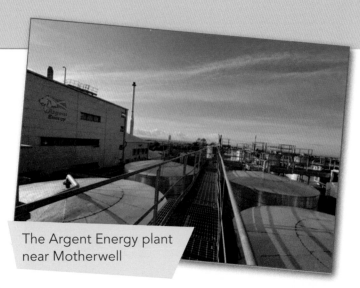

The Argent Energy plant near Motherwell

Home-made biodiesel

Some people have tried to make their own biodiesel in garages or sheds, often with disastrous consequences. However, you can make small quantities of it safely in a school science laboratory. If you make some, it may be possible to compare the properties of the biodiesel with those of the oil it was made from. For example, you could compare their viscosities, how easy they are to set on fire, how smoky their flames are and by how much an equal volume of each can heat up an equal volume of water.

Alcohol fuel

Ethanol (C_2H_5OH) can be produced from glucose. The glucose is fermented using the enzyme zymase, found in yeast, to produce ethanol.

glucose → ethanol + carbon dioxide

$$C_6H_{12}O_6(aq) \rightarrow 2C_2H_5OH(l) + 2CO_2(g)$$

The glucose used in this process is produced from sugar cane, therefore ethanol is a **renewable fuel**. Ethanol can be mixed with petrol to produce a cleaner-burning fuel. Burning ethanol does produce carbon dioxide but in lower quantities than regular petrol. Initially ethanol was used and exported as an alcohol fuel in Brazil but several other countries including Japan, China and the USA all widely use alcohol fuels now.

Biogas (green methane)

Methane can be obtained by methods other than the fractional distillation of crude oil or from natural gas. Organic waste (such as animal manure, human sewage and domestic refuse) can be fermented **anaerobically** (without oxygen) to produce methane. Methane produced this way is commonly referred to as **biogas**.

The major disadvantage of using biogas as a fuel is that because it is a hydrocarbon, it will still produce carbon dioxide and water on combustion.

biogas + oxygen → carbon dioxide + water

Although not widely used as an alternative to petrol, some European countries have taken biogas on board using it to power buses and even trains! Biogas can be considered a renewable fuel as it does not rely on using up our planet's finite resources. Raw biogas produced from digestion is unsuitable

QUESTIONS

1 Write a balanced chemical equation for the combustion of biogas (CH_4) to produce carbon dioxide and water.

2 Draw up a table listing the possible advantages and disadvantages of using biogas as a fuel.

3 ➗ Raw biogas produced from digestion contains 60% methane, 29% carbon dioxide and traces of other substances including hydrogen sulphide. Represent the chemical composition of raw biogas as a bar graph.

4 Methanol is another type of alcohol that can be used as an alcohol fuel. Use the internet to find out how methanol is obtained and some of the problems that make it unsuitable for regular use as a fuel.

for use as a fuel as it contains traces of **corrosive** hydrogen sulphide (H_2S). The biogas is **scrubbed** with water to produce a cleaner, safer fuel.

Hydrogen

Electrolysis of water using solar energy (which is a renewable source) produces hydrogen. Some people consider hydrogen to be a pollution-free energy source since water is the only product when hydrogen reacts with oxygen:

$$H_2(g) + \tfrac{1}{2}O_2(g) \rightarrow H_2O(l)$$

A spark or flame can cause this reaction. This is known as combustion, and it is a reaction which produces a lot of energy, mostly as heat and light. However, a **fuel cell** can also produce this energy without combusting the hydrogen and the energy produced is electrical. Currently, fuel cells are expensive, so although they can be used in vehicles which have been designed and built to run without burning fuels, most people will continue to use vehicles which burn petrol or diesel fuel.

In the UK, the Royal Mail commissioned three hydrogen vehicles to be used in trials delivering letters and packages in an effort to reduce their carbon emissions. One of the locations chosen for the initial trial was Stornoway on the Isle of Lewis in the Outer Hebrides of Scotland. They have set themselves the target of cutting carbon emissions by 50% before 2015 and are working on using hydrogen-powered double-decker delivery trucks which will be able to carry greater loads.

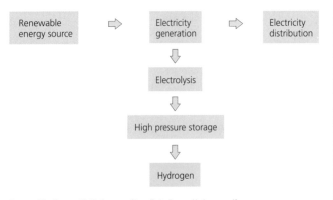
Filling up with hydrogen

Hydrogen could be produced in the following way without relying on fossil fuels.

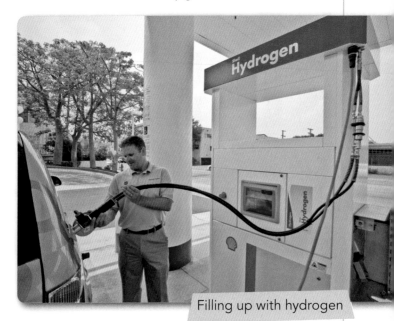

Source: http://www.cifalfindhorn.org/docs/Rob_Evans_Hydrogen.pdf

The solution for pollution?

Pollution-free fuels?

QUESTIONS

1 In the flowchart on page 99 electricity produced from a renewable source is used for electrolysis. What is being electrolysed and where could this be sourced from?

2 ➕➖✖➗ The Stornoway hydrogen fuel trial initially produced these statistics.

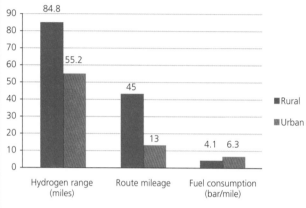

Source: http://www.cifalfindhorn.org/docs/Rob_Evans_Hydrogen.pdf

a) Why do you think fuel consumption is higher in urban areas than in rural areas?

b) If a postman in a rural area delivers on 6 days each week, how many full tanks of hydrogen fuel would he use?

c) How much hydrogen fuel (in bar) would be used on a single delivery in an urban area?

3 Find out exactly what 'carbon emissions' means.

4 📖 Research Cenex, the UK's first Centre for Excellence for low carbon and fuel cell technologies. Find out about some current alternative fuel initiatives. Prepare a short report for local business owners encouraging them to move to renewable fuels.

GLOSSARY

Base a chemical that will neutralise an acid

Combustion a reaction between a material and oxygen which releases energy

Corrosive a substance that will react by 'eating through' surfaces and can cause destruction or damage to living tissues

Electrolysis breaking up of a chemical compound using electricity

Fossil fuels fuels formed from the anaerobic decomposition of plant and animal material buried for millions of years (such as coal, oil, natural gas and peat)

Hypoxic lacking oxygen

Neutralisation a type of chemical reaction between an acid and a base in which the pH moves towards 7

Particulate matter small particles of a solid or liquid that are dispersed throughout a liquid or gas as a form of pollution

Renewable fuel a fuel which is produced from renewable resources and so is not a drain on finite resources such as fossil fuels

Scrubbed cleansed of impurities

MATERIALS
Properties and uses of substances

9

What's new in the material world?

Level 3   What came before?

 SCN 3-16a

I can differentiate between pure substances and mixtures in common use and can select appropriate physical methods for separating mixtures into their components.

Level 4   What is this chapter about?

 SCN 4-16a

I have carried out research into novel materials and can begin to explain the scientific basis of their properties and discuss the possible impact they may have on society.

What's new in the material world?

Early materials

For thousands of years, humans only had access to natural materials. Clothes were made from wool, fur, leather, cotton, linen or silk. Parcels were wrapped in brown paper and tied with string. Food was sold loose or, at best, wrapped in greaseproof paper. Poor people wore wooden shoes. Rubber was harvested from trees and the few raincoats available were made from waxed cotton or oiled animal skins.

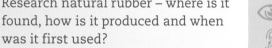

Active Learning ▶

Research natural rubber – where is it found, how is it produced and when was it first used?

The birth of a consumer society

In only 100 years, science has changed everything. Cheap, easily available energy (electricity and gas) has made our lives warm and comfortable, but more importantly, cheap energy has encouraged the discovery and mass production of new materials. These days we are all **consumers** and consumers demand both **convenience** and novelty. This demand has sent the rate of scientific discovery into overdrive. The speed at which new ideas are being proposed, discussed, tested, then either discarded or put into practice, is breath-taking.

Novel materials

Research into **novel materials** focuses on improving the performance of materials, such as plastics, metals and **ceramics**, by altering their structures to give them new properties for a wide range of products and applications. In this chapter we will look at a few of the new novel materials that were developed in the late twentieth and early twenty-first centuries, but we will start with a type of substance you already know about from Chapter 3: alloys.

Alloys

An alloy is a mixture of a metal and one or more other elements (usually other metals). Alloys have been used for thousands of years. They are designed to have particular properties so they can do a specific job. For example, stainless steel (iron + carbon + chromium) does not rust and solder (tin + lead) has a low melting point and is harder than either tin or lead.

One recently invented group of alloys share a quite spectacular property. These are known as **shape memory alloys** (SMAs). These metal mixtures can 'remember' their original shape and when they are heated above a certain temperature (the transition temperature), they will return to that shape no matter how much they have been bent or folded. They do this because atoms in a piece of metal are arranged in a particular way (we say metals have a crystal structure) and at their transition temperature, SMAs change from one type of crystal structure to another. When they change their structure, they change their shape. The first SMAs were nickel–titanium alloys but there are now many different SMAs with widely varying transition temperatures and uses.

Some uses of shape memory alloys

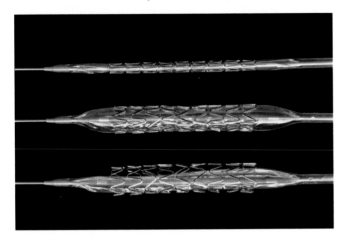

Stents are devices used to hold open clogged arteries, usually around the heart. SMA stents are very thin pieces of metal which are inserted into a big artery in the thigh and pushed all the way up the artery to the correct position near the heart. They have a transition temperature close to body temperature, so when they are in position, the shape changes to a coil or cylinder which holds the artery open. The surgeon has to work pretty fast!

Fire alarm sprinkler systems use SMAs with high transition temperatures. When a fire raises the temperature, the originally curved contact straightens, breaks the circuit and triggers the sprinklers.

GPS and **mobile phone satellites** have aerials with a big surface area. These would be damaged during launch so they are folded on SMA frames which open out when the satellite is in orbit and exposure to the Sun's rays has made them reach their transition temperatures.

Active Learning ▶

Use the internet to find out what 'smart materials' are and find out how artists and designers are using them.

Novel materials

Titanium dioxide

Titanium dioxide (also called titania, chemical formula TiO_2) is a remarkably versatile compound which has been used for many years as a pigment in white paint. However, titania is also a material that can absorb the part of the Sun's rays that causes tanning and sunburn (light of **wavelength** less than 400 nanometres). For this reason, **nano-particles** of titanium dioxide are used in a lot of sunscreen creams and lotions. Nano-particles are very tiny (in the region of 1×10^{-9} metres in diameter) – science at this scale is called **nanoscience**. Their size means that a very small mass of titanium dioxide particles has a very big surface area and can absorb a lot of harmful radiation.

Titania also acts as a **photocatalyst**, a chemical that absorbs light and uses the energy to speed up chemical reactions. Grease reacts with oxygen according to the equation:

$$grease + O_2 \rightarrow CO_2 + H_2O$$

This reaction happens very, very slowly all the time, but in the presence of titania, it happens quite fast, giving what is called a 'cold **combustion**' reaction. It is mainly the greasy, organic deposits on glass that dirt and dust stick to, making windows dirty. Advances in **nanotechnology**

have allowed scientists to coat window surfaces with a 30-nanometre thick layer of titanium dioxide (30 nm is about 1/50 000th the thickness of a human hair), so sunlight comes through the glass and no-one can see the titania layer. The photocatalyst speeds up the breakdown of grease, then rain washes the dust off the windows. This is sold as 'self-cleaning' glass and although it is not perfect, as long as it is washed with regular showers of rain, it stays a lot cleaner than normal glass.

Titania might also be useful in the search for new energy sources. As a photocatalyst, it can use solar energy to catalyse the splitting of water into hydrogen and oxygen. This was first investigated by Japanese researchers in the 1970s, and in the past ten years, Honda has put money into the development of a cell where a TiO_2/Pt (titania/platinum) photocatalyst uses sunlight to produce hydrogen. Scientists have thousands of ideas; most do not go anywhere and are discarded, but some lead to revolutionary developments. The trick is to spot the good ideas!

QUESTIONS

1 What does the word 'pigment' mean?

2 What is the approximate size of an atom in nanometres (nm)?

3 What range of wavelengths in the electromagnetic spectrum can we see?

4 Why is the reaction of grease with oxygen called a cold combustion reaction?

5 If the compounds CO_2 and H_2O are produced when grease reacts with oxygen, which elements must be present in grease?

6 If the formula for titanium dioxide is TiO_2, what is the valency of titanium in this compound?

Carbon fibres

One of the materials used in the body of a Grand Prix racing car is **carbon fibre** or, more accurately, carbon fibres because these days there are a lot of different varieties. Carbon fibres are also found in skis, tennis racquets and aeroplane engines because the materials that we call 'carbon fibres' are very light, very strong and do not expand much when they are heated. Carbon fibres were first made in the 1950s in America, but most of the early development work was done in the UK. Only one UK-based carbon fibre manufacturing company survived past the 1990s, however, and that is a Scottish company, formerly RK Carbon Fibres Ltd, based in Ross-shire, now known as SGL.

Carbon fibres are mainly made from **polymers** (giant molecules) like poly(acrylonitrile), commonly called PAN.

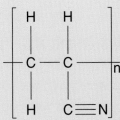

The repeat unit for a PAN molecule: the polymer consists of this section of the chain repeated n times, where n is a number between 2000 and 20 000

Active Learning ▶

1 Investigate recent developments at SGL.

2 Find out which parts of a Formula One car are made from carbon fibre materials. What are the advantages and disadvantages of using these materials in a racing car?

3 One nanometre (nm) is 1×10^{-9} metre. Find out what a micrometre (μm) is in metres.

The polymer is stretched so that the molecules lie more or less parallel to each other.	Heat treatment to remove non-carbon atoms — This leaves thin fibres (about 6–10 micrometres) that are around 90% carbon.	The fibres are twisted into threads then woven into sheets, tubes or any shape that is required.	The fibres are then embedded in plastic (called **resin**), moulded to shape and then baked.

Carbon fibre resin is much stronger than either the carbon or the resin on its own: the carbon fibres reinforce the plastic resin in the same way that putting straw into bricks or steel rods into concrete reinforces those materials.

What's new in the material world?

Novel materials

Fullerenes and nanotubes

Carbon is a very versatile element and it exists in a variety of different solid forms. The most recently discovered are called diamond **nanorods**, but the most stable forms are graphite, diamond and **fullerenes**. The carbon atoms in fullerenes have similar bonding to the carbon atoms in graphite, but the flat graphite sheets are curved in fullerenes to make hollow balls (fullerenes) and tubes (nanotubes).

graphite   diamond   buckyball

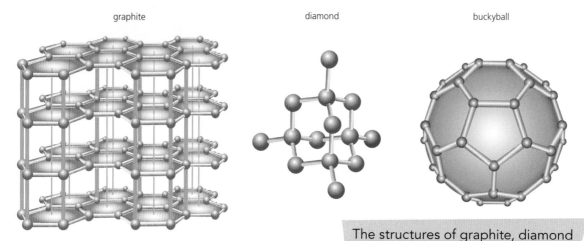

The structures of graphite, diamond and C_{60}, the 'buckyball'

Graphite is made up entirely of hexagons of carbon atoms. Fullerenes have a curved shape because they consist of a mixture of connected pentagons and hexagons of carbon atoms. Buckminsterfullerene (C_{60}), the most stable fullerene, commonly called a buckyball, gets its 'soccer ball' shape by joining twelve pentagons with twenty hexagons. That sounds like 180 carbon atoms [$(12 \times 5) + (20 \times 6)$], but each carbon atom is part of more than one pentagon or hexagon! You can see this in the diagram above and, if you need more convincing, you can make a buckyball later in the chapter.

Fullerenes were discovered by Harry Kroto at Sussex University in the mid 1980s. He and two American scientists were given the 1996 Nobel Prize for Chemistry for their work on fullerenes. **Nanotubes** were discovered by a Japanese scientist in the early 1990s and in the last decade they have become very important, especially in nanotechnology. Nanotubes have some quite remarkable properties. Their ability to conduct electricity depends on the diameter of the tube: they can be either **semiconducting** or metallic depending on their size. The bonds which form between carbon atoms are some of the strongest bonds in nature and this makes nanotubes very strong. For example, a nanotube device has been made which recorded a strength of about 220 times that of steel. Despite their strength, they are flexible and elastic so they are being developed for use as probes in scanning tunnelling microscopes.

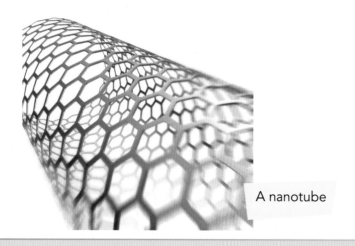

A nanotube

Graphene

Two scientists working at Manchester University won the 2010 Nobel Prize in Physics for their work on **graphene**. At present it seems that graphene is the end of the line in terms of size of carbon structures. Graphene is a unique, two-dimensional material that has a huge surface area to mass ratio. It is a single 'sheet' from a piece of graphite – a layer of carbon that is only one atom thick. It is the thinnest, yet the strongest material known.

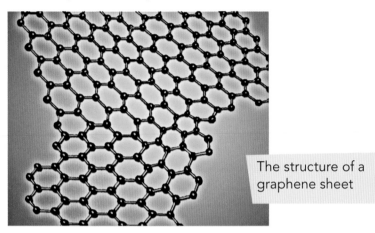

The structure of a graphene sheet

Graphene is completely transparent, a good conductor of electricity and an excellent conductor of heat. Its properties and possible uses are still being investigated, but graphene makes nanotubes look big and clumsy. If it can be used in place of carbon fibres (to reinforce plastic) and in place of nanotubes (to make micro-transistors) another new generation of materials could be on the horizon.

Active Learning ▶

1 Using thin card, cut out twelve regular pentagons and twenty regular hexagons with the same side lengths and use them to make a model of a buckyball.

2 Research the work of a man called Richard Buckminster Fuller.

3 What is the formula mass of a C_{70} fullerene?

4 Look on the internet and find out how many carbon atoms are in a) the smallest known fullerene and b) the largest known fullerene.

5 Research the work of the Vega Science Trust (www.vega.org.uk) set up by Harry Kroto in the mid 1990s.

6 Harry Kroto was awarded honorary degrees by a number of universities in recognition of his achievements. Find out why he returned them in protest to the University of Hertfordshire in 2001 and the University of Exeter in 2004. Do you agree with his reasons?

GLOSSARY

Ceramics substances, usually made of some sort of clay, which stay permanently hard after they have been heated

Combustion a reaction between a material and oxygen which releases energy

Consumers people buying goods and services for their own use

Convenience freedom from effort due to having a useful or helpful device

Fullerene a form of the element carbon where the atoms combine to make sheets of hexagons and pentagons which then roll up to make hollow spheres

GPS global positioning system; satellites in orbit around the planet which transmit information telling us exactly where we are on the surface of the Earth

Nanoscience the study of materials that have remarkable properties because of their very small size – in the region of 1×10^{-9} metres

Nanotechnology the application of nanoscience to just about all areas of research; all substances have a surface and nanoscience allows us to look at, among other things, surface atoms

Nanotube similar to a fullerene, but the sheets of carbon atoms roll up to make tubes containing around 70 (or more) carbon atoms

Novel material any substance that is interestingly new and unusual

Polymer a giant molecule made by joining together thousands of smaller molecules (monomers)

Semiconductor a substance which conducts electricity above a certain applied voltage, but does not conduct if the voltage applied across it is below a certain value

Wavelength the distance between each successive crest of an electromagnetic wave; used to identify where in the spectrum a sound, light or radio wave is located

Index

Index

Curriculum for Excellence mapping grid

Curriculum for Excellence Science Level 4 Experiences and Outcomes

Category	Experiences and Outcomes	Chapter 1	Chapter 2	Chapter 3	Chapter 4	Chapter 5	Chapter 6	Chapter 7	Chapter 8	Chapter 9
Planet Earth	SCN 4-01a									
	SCN 4-02a									
	SCN 4-02b									
	SCN 4-03a								■	
	SCN 4-04a								■	
	SCN 4-04b		■	■						
	SCN 4-05a									
	SCN 4-05b							■		
	SCN 4-06a									
Forces, Electricity and Waves	SCN 4-07a									
	SCN 4-07b									
	SCN 4-08a									
	SCN 4-08b									
	SCN 4-09a									
	SCN 4-09b									
	SCN 4-09c									
	SCN 4-10a				■					
	SCN 4-10b				■					
	SCN 4-11a									
	SCN 4-11b									
Biological Systems	SCN 4-12a									
	SCN 4-12b									
	SCN 4-13a									
	SCN 4-13b									
	SCN 4-13c									
	SCN 4-14a									
	SCN 4-14b									
	SCN 4-14c									
Materials	SCN 4-15a	■								
	SCN 4-16a									■
	SCN 4-16b						■			
	SCN 4-17a		■							
	SCN 4-18a								■	
	SCN 4-19a					■				
	SCN 4-19b			■						
Topical Science	SCN 4-20a									
	SCN 4-20b							■		